First World War
and Army of Occupation
War Diary
France, Belgium and Germany

31 DIVISION
Divisional Troops
Divisional Signal Company
1 April 1916 - 26 February 1919

WO95/2352/4

The Naval & Military Press Ltd
www.nmarchive.com
Published in association with The National Archives

Published by

The Naval & Military Press Ltd

Unit 10 Ridgewood Industrial Park,

Uckfield, East Sussex,

TN22 5QE England

Tel: +44 (0) 1825 749494

www.naval-military-press.com

www.nmarchive.com

This diary has been reprinted in facsimile from the original. Any imperfections are inevitably reproduced and the quality may fall short of modern type and cartographic standards.

© **Crown Copyright**
Images reproduced by permission of The National Archives, London, England, 2015.

Contents

Document type	Place/Title	Date From	Date To
Heading	WO95/2352/4		
Heading	31st Division 31st Divl Signal Coy R.E. Apr 1916-Feb 1919		
War Diary	Bus-Les Artois	01/04/1916	17/04/1916
War Diary	Bus.	18/04/1916	30/04/1916
Diagram etc	Signal Office 31 Divisional Signal Coy. Royal Engineers Bus.		
Diagram etc	Traffic Record		
War Diary	Bus Les Artois	01/06/1916	14/06/1916
War Diary	Bus	15/06/1916	30/06/1916
Diagram etc	Cable Scheme. H.C.O.		
Heading	War Diary 31 Divisional Signal Coy R.E. July 1916 Vol 5		
War Diary	Bus	01/07/1916	05/07/1916
War Diary	Ribeaucourt	06/07/1916	08/07/1916
War Diary	St Venant	09/07/1916	15/07/1916
War Diary	Lestrem	15/07/1916	31/07/1916
Miscellaneous	Communications. General. Throughout The Operation. Appendix 6		
Miscellaneous	Bombardment. (Telephone And Telegraph).		
Miscellaneous	Consolidation Of Objective.		
Miscellaneous	Visual.		
Miscellaneous	Runners.		
Miscellaneous	Pigeon Service.		
Miscellaneous	Wireless		
Miscellaneous	Appendix 1		
Miscellaneous	Appendix 2		
Miscellaneous	Brief Report On Communications During Operation On July 1st 1916. Appendix 7	01/07/1916	01/07/1916
Heading	War Diary Of 31st Divl Signal Coy August 1916. Vol 6		
War Diary	Lestrem	01/08/1916	31/08/1916
Diagram etc	Communications 31st Div Lestrem. Appendix 8		
Diagram etc	Traffic Record. Appendix 9		
Heading	War Diary 31st Divisional Signal Coy. Royal Engineers September 1916. Vol 7		
War Diary	Lestrem	01/09/1916	17/09/1916
War Diary	Locon	18/09/1916	30/09/1916
Diagram etc	App 10 A.		
Diagram etc	App 10 B.		
Diagram etc	Traffic Record September 1916. Appendix 11		
Heading	War Diary. 31st Divisional Signal Coy R.E. October 1916. Vol 8		
War Diary	Locon	01/10/1916	07/10/1916
War Diary	Marieux	08/10/1916	16/10/1916
War Diary	Authie	17/10/1916	31/10/1916
Operation(al) Order(s)	Supplementary Instructions 'A' To 31st Division Order No. 69. Appendix 12		
Diagram etc	Communications 31st Div.-Sailly Quarries Occupied As Advanced Div. H.Q. Appendix 13		
Diagram etc	Traffic Record October 1916		

Heading	War Diary. 31st Divisional Signal Coy. R.E. November 1916 Vol 9		
War Diary	Authie	01/11/1916	30/11/1916
Diagram etc	Traffic Record November 1916. App 14		
Heading	War Diary. 31st Divisional Signal Coy. R.E. December Vol 10		
War Diary	Couin	01/12/1916	31/12/1916
Diagram etc	Traffic Record December 1916. App 16		
Heading	War Diary 31st Divisional Signal Company R.E. January 1917. Vol XI.		
War Diary	Couin	01/01/1917	11/01/1917
War Diary	Beauval	11/01/1917	21/01/1917
War Diary	Bernaville	22/01/1917	31/01/1917
Heading	Traffic Record. January 1917. App 17		
Heading	War Diary 31st Divisional Signal Coy. R.E. February 1917. Vol 12		
War Diary	Bernaville	01/02/1917	19/02/1917
War Diary	Beauval	20/02/1917	20/02/1917
War Diary	Authie	21/02/1917	28/02/1917
Diagram etc	Traffic Record February 1917. App 18		
Diagram etc	YCA Communications Feb-March 1917. App 19		
Heading	War Diary. 31st Divisional Signal Company. R.E. March 1917. Vol 13		
War Diary	Authie	01/03/1917	03/03/1917
War Diary	Couin	04/03/1917	19/03/1917
War Diary	Bouquemaison	20/03/1917	20/03/1917
War Diary	Ramecourt	21/03/1917	21/03/1917
War Diary	Pernes	22/03/1917	23/03/1917
War Diary	Norrent Fontes	24/03/1917	24/03/1917
War Diary	St. Venant	25/03/1917	31/03/1917
Diagram etc	Traffic Record March 1917. Appendix 20		
Heading	War Diary. 31st Divisional Signal Coy. R.E. April 1917. Vol 14		
War Diary	St. Venant	01/04/1917	10/04/1917
War Diary	Bruay	11/04/1917	14/04/1917
War Diary	Ourton	15/04/1917	28/04/1917
War Diary	Villers Chatel	29/04/1917	29/04/1917
War Diary	About 2 1/2 Miles NE Of Arrives	30/04/1917	30/04/1917
Diagram etc	Traffic Record April 1917		
Heading	War Diary. 31st Divisional Signal Company R.E. May 1917. Vol 15		
War Diary	Nr Roclincourt	01/05/1917	21/05/1917
War Diary	Villers Chatel	22/05/1917	31/05/1917
Operation(al) Order(s)	Signal Instructions In Conjunction With 31st Division Order No. 139. Appendix No. 22	02/05/1917	02/05/1917
Miscellaneous	Division Exchange.		
Miscellaneous	OP. Exch. For Div. Arty.		
Miscellaneous	Report On Communications During Operations May 3rd. Divisional.	03/05/1917	03/05/1917
Miscellaneous	92nd Brigade Sector.		
Miscellaneous	Artillery Communications.		
Miscellaneous	Summary And Suggestions.	10/05/1917	10/05/1917
Diagram etc	Forward Communications 31st Division Key Diagram		
Miscellaneous	Details of Defense Signal Communications 31st Division.	18/05/1917	18/05/1917

Miscellaneous	Details of Communication Arrangements in 31st Division Area.		
Miscellaneous	Right Brigade Rear Headquarters.		
Miscellaneous	HQ 223rd F.A. Brigade.		
Miscellaneous	V Test Points.		
Miscellaneous	Rear Communications.		
Miscellaneous	Y.C.A. Circuits.		
Miscellaneous	Map Reference 51B. Telegraph Circulation.		
Heading	War Diary. 31st Divisional Signal Company R.E. June 1917. Vol 16		
War Diary	Villers Chatel	01/06/1917	10/06/1917
War Diary	Nr. Roclincourt	11/06/1917	18/06/1917
War Diary	Roclincourt	19/06/1917	30/06/1917
Miscellaneous	Appendix "C" Signal Arrangements.		
Miscellaneous	Report On Communications During Operations On June 28th 1917. Appendix 24	28/06/1917	28/06/1917
Diagram etc	Traffic Record. June 1917. App 25		
Heading	War Diary 31st Divisional Signal Coy. R.E. July 1917. Vol 17		
War Diary	Roclincourt	01/07/1917	04/07/1917
War Diary	Villers Chatel	04/07/1917	13/07/1917
War Diary	Fort George	14/07/1917	31/07/1917
Diagram etc	Traffic Record July 1917		
War Diary	Fort George	01/08/1917	25/08/1917
War Diary	F.12.A.5.5	26/08/1917	31/08/1917
Diagram etc	Traffic Record August 1917		
Heading	War Diary. Headquarters 31st Divisional Signal Coy. September 1917 Vol 19		
War Diary	F.12.A.5.5	01/09/1917	06/09/1917
War Diary	A.2.9.A.3.4	07/09/1917	30/09/1917
Diagram etc	Traffic Record September 1917		
Heading	War Diary. 31st Divisional Signal Coy R.E. October 1917. Vol 20		
War Diary	A.2.9.a.3.4	01/10/1917	31/10/1917
Heading	War Diary. 31st Divisional Signal Coy. R.E. November 1917 Vol 21		
War Diary	A.2.9.A.3.4. Nr. Roclincourt	01/11/1917	30/11/1917
Heading	War Diary. 31st Divisional Signal Company. R.E. December 1917. Vol 22		
War Diary	A.2.9.A.3.4. Roclincourt	01/12/1917	11/12/1917
War Diary	Villers Chatel	12/12/1917	18/12/1917
War Diary	A.2.9.3.4. Roclincourt	19/12/1917	31/12/1917
Diagram etc	Traffic Record December 1917		
War Diary	A 29 A 34 Roclincourt	01/01/1918	28/02/1918
Heading	31st Divisional Engineers. War Diary 31st Divisional Signal Company March 1918		
War Diary	Roclincourt A 29 A 34	01/03/1918	03/03/1918
War Diary	Villers Chatel	04/03/1918	21/03/1918
War Diary	Basseux	22/03/1918	23/03/1918
War Diary	Ayette	23/03/1918	25/03/1918
War Diary	Humber Camps	25/03/1918	31/03/1918
Heading	31st Divisional Engineers 31st Divisional Signal Company R.E. April 1918		
Heading	War Diary Of April 1918. Vol 26		
War Diary	Humbercamps	01/04/1918	01/04/1918
War Diary	Lucheux	02/04/1918	02/04/1918

War Diary	Villers Chatel	03/04/1918	10/04/1918
War Diary	Vieux Berquin	11/04/1918	11/04/1918
War Diary	La Motte	11/04/1918	12/04/1918
War Diary	Le Gd Hasard	13/04/1918	14/04/1918
War Diary	Hondeghem	15/04/1918	18/04/1918
War Diary	Wallon Cappel	19/04/1918	27/04/1918
War Diary	Hondeghem	28/04/1918	30/04/1918
Miscellaneous			
Heading	War Diary 31st Division Signal Coy. From 1st To 31st May 1918. Vol. 27		
War Diary	Hondeghem	01/05/1918	31/05/1918
Miscellaneous	Appendix A. Subscribers 31 Div Hqrs Exchange.	02/05/1918	02/05/1918
Miscellaneous	31st Divisional Signal Coy. Appendix B.		
Miscellaneous			
Miscellaneous	Messenger Dogs. Appendix C.		
War Diary	Wardrecques	01/06/1918	15/06/1918
War Diary	Ebblinghem.	16/06/1918	17/06/1918
War Diary	Wardrecques	18/06/1918	30/06/1918
War Diary	Wardrecques	22/06/1918	27/06/1918
Miscellaneous	Communications For "Borderland" Divisional. Appendix A.		
Miscellaneous	92nd Brigade Communications.		
Miscellaneous	Artillery Communications.		
Diagram etc	Communications Borderland		
Miscellaneous	93rd Infantry Brigade Communications For The Attack On Ankle Farm 27.6.18. Appendix A.	27/06/1918	27/06/1918
Miscellaneous	Notes On Communication During Borderland Operations. Appendix A.		
Miscellaneous	Notes On Communications Of 31 Bn Machine Gun Corps During Borderland Operations. Appendix A.		
War Diary	Wallon Cappel	01/07/1918	31/08/1918
Miscellaneous	Subscribers on Telephone Exchanges in 31st Divisional Area. Appendix A.	27/08/1918	27/08/1918
War Diary		01/09/1918	06/09/1918
War Diary		05/09/1918	31/10/1918
War Diary	Courtrai	01/11/1918	10/11/1918
War Diary	Ruyen Renaix	11/11/1918	14/11/1918
War Diary	Courtrai	15/11/1918	24/11/1918
War Diary	St. Omer	25/11/1918	30/11/1918
War Diary	Blendecques	01/12/1918	11/01/1919
War Diary	Bailleul		
War Diary	Calais	29/01/1919	31/01/1919
War Diary	Bailleul	06/02/1919	06/02/1919
War Diary	Blendecques	06/02/1919	26/02/1919

31ST DIVISION

31ST DIVL SIGNAL COY. R.E.
APR 1916 - FEB 1919

31ST DIVISION

Army Form C. 2118

WAR DIARY
or
INTELLIGENCE SUMMARY 3/1st DIV. SIGNAL Coy R.E.

(Erase heading not required.)

April 1916

Place	Date	Hour	Summary of Events and Information	Remarks and references to Appendices
BUS-les-ARTOIS	April 1st		Same communication as on last day of March. Took over "Beaussart" Artillery Exchange from 36th Division. Traffic 682.	
"	2nd to 11th		Tracing Cuis, of which no stable diagram was obtainable, was main work during this period. As this division was taking over battle from 48th and 36th Divisions and had to be laid. The difficulty being that the 36th Artillery Wire covering 31st Infantry Cuis and that when the 31st Infantry head were relieved by Infantry of 29th Divn the 31st Artillery remained covering a portion of 29th Divn Front, until the 29th Artillery went into the Line.	
"	12th		92nd Bde was due at COLIN CAMP. 94th Bde to BERTRANCOURT. 93rd Bde to BUS. Artillery remaining in action covering 36th Div front at MAILLY and ENGLEBELMER. Opened telegraph to Infantry Brigades and 6th R'jing Telephones. Artillery communications remaining as previously.	App A.
"	14th		Commenced to move into new Signal Office, especially built near the Divisional Head Quarters Offices. Plan of Office in App. A.	
"	15th		Commenced to bury cables. 600 men being allotted daily. Trenches being made 4 foot deep. The Scheme being to bury all cables between 3'5-0" & 4'0" of the Front line.	
"	16th		Commenced a "Course of Instruction" for Artillery Battery Brigade Battery Officers in Communication. Syllabus of Course attached in Appendix B.	App B
"	17th		BEAUSSART ARTILLERY exchange handed to 29th Div. Artillery, with drew from ENGLEBELMER and "Group" H.Q. Established at COLIN CAMP. Signed off to the Group of the 6th Infantry Telephone to them, Telegrams being sent with by the Infantry Brigade H.Q. there.	

Army Form C. 2118

WAR DIARY
or
INTELLIGENCE SUMMARY

(Erase heading not required.)

Place	Date	Hour	Summary of Events and Information	Remarks and references to Appendices
BUS.	April 18th		Commenced "Corps Cable Trench Scheme" E9: To bury all cables 6 foot deep. 400 men per day allotted for this work. Suspended temporarily the divisional scheme in order to save labour and to make it fit into the Corps Scheme.	
"	19th		2/LIEUT CARD R.E. attached from 8th Corps Signals to assist in buried cable scheme.	
"	20th		Adopted the system of having No 2 Section Linesmen permanently in the line to be in charge of "Al Queer" communications. It was found that with each Brigade changing every 8 days, the Signal Section going into the line hardly had time to learn the wires before coming out.	
"	21st to 30th		No changes in communication - The normal Brigade reliefs every 8 days taking place.	
			Appendix C gives diagram of traffic throughout the month	App C

Major
Officer Comdg.
3rd Signal Coy.

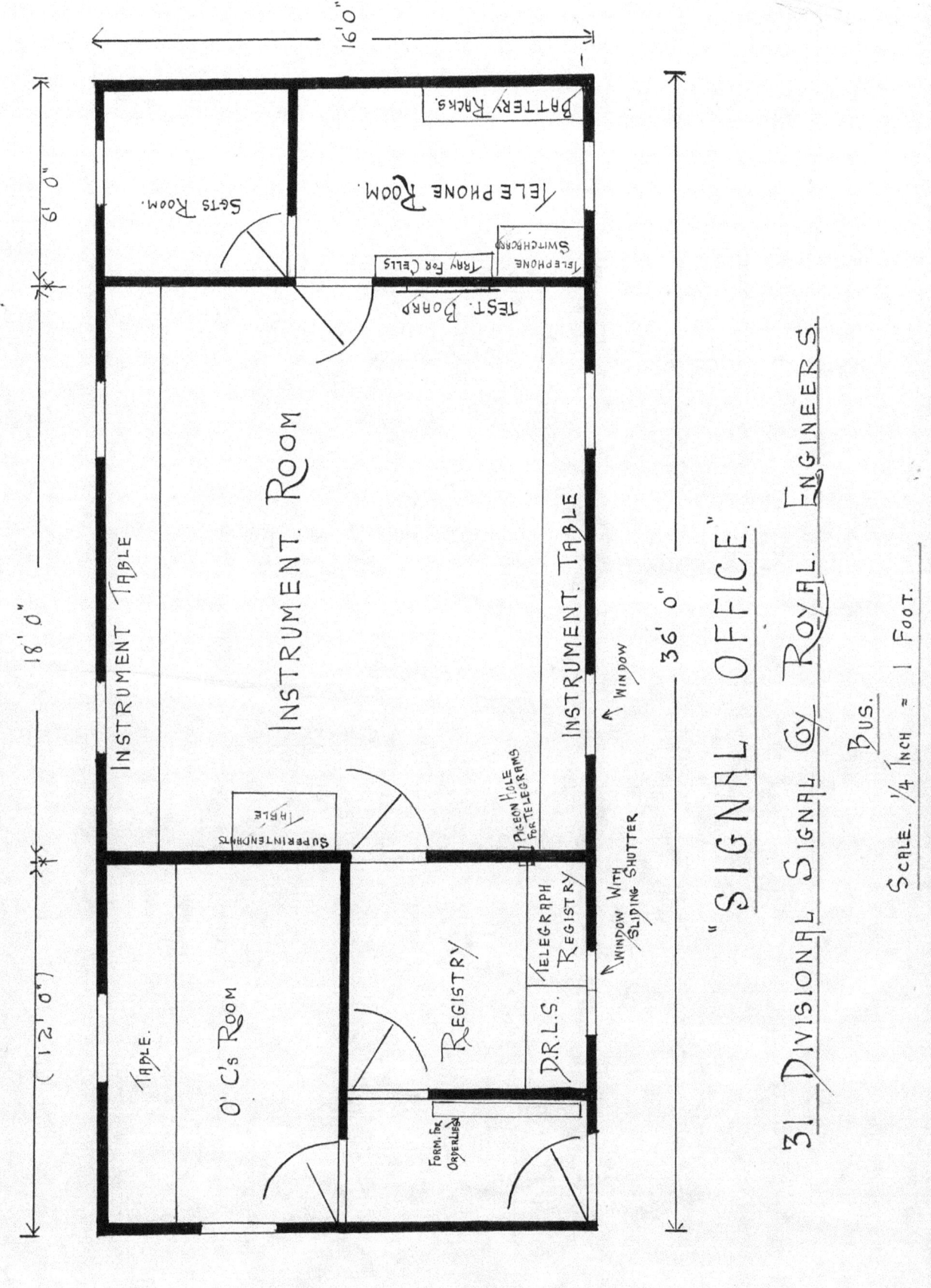

TRAFFIC RECORD
1ST TO 30TH APRIL 1916.
FOR
31 DIVISIONAL SIGNAL COY R.E.

— Telegrams.
— Sealed Packets
— Total Telegrams & S.P.s

MAY
~~JUNE~~

31 / vol 3.4

31st DIV. SIGNAL COY.

Army Form C. 2118

WAR DIARY
or
INTELLIGENCE SUMMARY
(Erase heading not required.)

Instructions regarding War Diaries and Intelligence Summaries are contained in F. S. Regs., Part II. and the Staff Manual respectively. Title Pages will be prepared in manuscript.

Place	Date	Hour	Summary of Events and Information	Remarks and references to Appendices
BUS les ARTOIS	May 1st to 10th		Working on buried Cable Scheme; digging trenches in accordance with task sheets by Sig. Coy. Constructing airline to COURCELLES. Other work normal and regular.	
	May 10th to 30th		Nothing of interest to bring to notice. Working of Cable trunks Experiencing difficulty owing to the frequent changing of artillery OP positions. Normal Brigade reliefs every 8 days. Traffic normal about 400 telegrams daily. A continual increase in telephone traffic and demand for more bell ringing telephones.	

Lieut Capt. Coy.
31 Div Signal Coy.

Army Form C. 2118

WAR DIARY
or
INTELLIGENCE SUMMARY

(Erase heading not required.)

31st Div. Signal Coy. R.E.

Place	Date JUNE	Hour	Summary of Events and Information	Remarks and references to Appendices
BUS les ARTOIS	1st		Carrid registering at "closed" packets, also keeping record of these marked "R".	
	2nd		Commenced laying the Corps cable trenches with the object of using the lines for immediate defensive purposes.	
	3rd		Others in buried cables to "Left Sector" (i.e. Left Battalion Hq in the line)	
			" " " "Right Sector". (i.e. right and centre Battalion.)	
	4th		Front rearranged, one brigade (93rd) holding the line with 3 battalions	
	5th		93rd Bde HQ at Colincamps holding the line with 3 battalions. 94th Bde from COURCELLES to GEZAINCOURT. Telegraph and telephone communication being maintained via 8th Corps. 31st Div Supply Column move from BEAUQUESNE to SARTON.	
	6th		31st Train moves from VAUCHELLES to AUTHIE. Telephone lines borrowed from 8th Corps.	
	7th		Laying Cable Trenches.	
	8th		Multicore cable obtained by 8th Corps for wiring cable trenches between dugouts.	
	9th		Digging and wiring cable trenches, to reduce the line to 10 days to that previously notified.	
	12th		Head at wiring had to be complete by 30th. Thanks to 8th Corps commenced laying multicore	
	13th		Digging and laying cables.	
	14th		Multicore being laid from "K" to "M" in this area. P.O. underground joints making at necessary connections to the dugouts. To drying	

Army Form C. 2118

WAR DIARY
or
INTELLIGENCE SUMMARY
(Erase heading not required.)

Instructions regarding War Diaries and Intelligence Summaries are contained in F.S. Regs., Part II. and the Staff Manual respectively. Title Pages will be prepared in manuscript.

Place	Date	Hour	Summary of Events and Information	Remarks and references to Appendices
BHS	JUNE 15.		Utensils & jointing tools available. Very wet weather the cable trenches fling in several places 4 feet deep in water.	App 1 to 5
"	16.		Laying multicore from M to N and from N - P & ? B	
"	17.		Fitting in trenches and testing circuits	
"	18/6 20.		"	
"	21.		"	
"	22.		"	
"	23.		All buried circuits working correct	
"	24.		Testing circuits & making final preparations	
"	.		Preliminary bombardment commenced. Three battery wires broken by direct hits by hostile shell. Repaired at night.	
"	25		Aeroplane dropped bomb near Signal Office Bus breaking 15 wires (airline) & hand telegraph to 165 ?A?B 170 ?A?B to relieve traffic & telephone lines	
"	26		3rd day of bombardment. All wires intact.	
"	27		4th day of bombardment - 3.20.05 cut off - Buy forward portion of forward spur cut.	

1875 Wt. W593/826 1,000,000 4/15 I.B.C. & A. A.D.S.S./Forms/C. 2118.

WAR DIARY
or
INTELLIGENCE SUMMARY

(Erase heading not required.)

Army Form C. 2118

Place	Date	Hour	Summary of Events and Information	Remarks and references to Appendices
25th July BUS	28th June		5th day of bombardment. Both wires to Southern Div O.P. broken 6pm. All other wires good. The assault postponed for 48 hours. Southern Div O.P. wires repaired	
	29th		6th day of bombardment. All lines correct.	
	30th	12 m.n.	Three infantry Brigade HQ in position at Battle H.Q. All lines correct.	

Major O/c
51 Div. Sig. Coy.

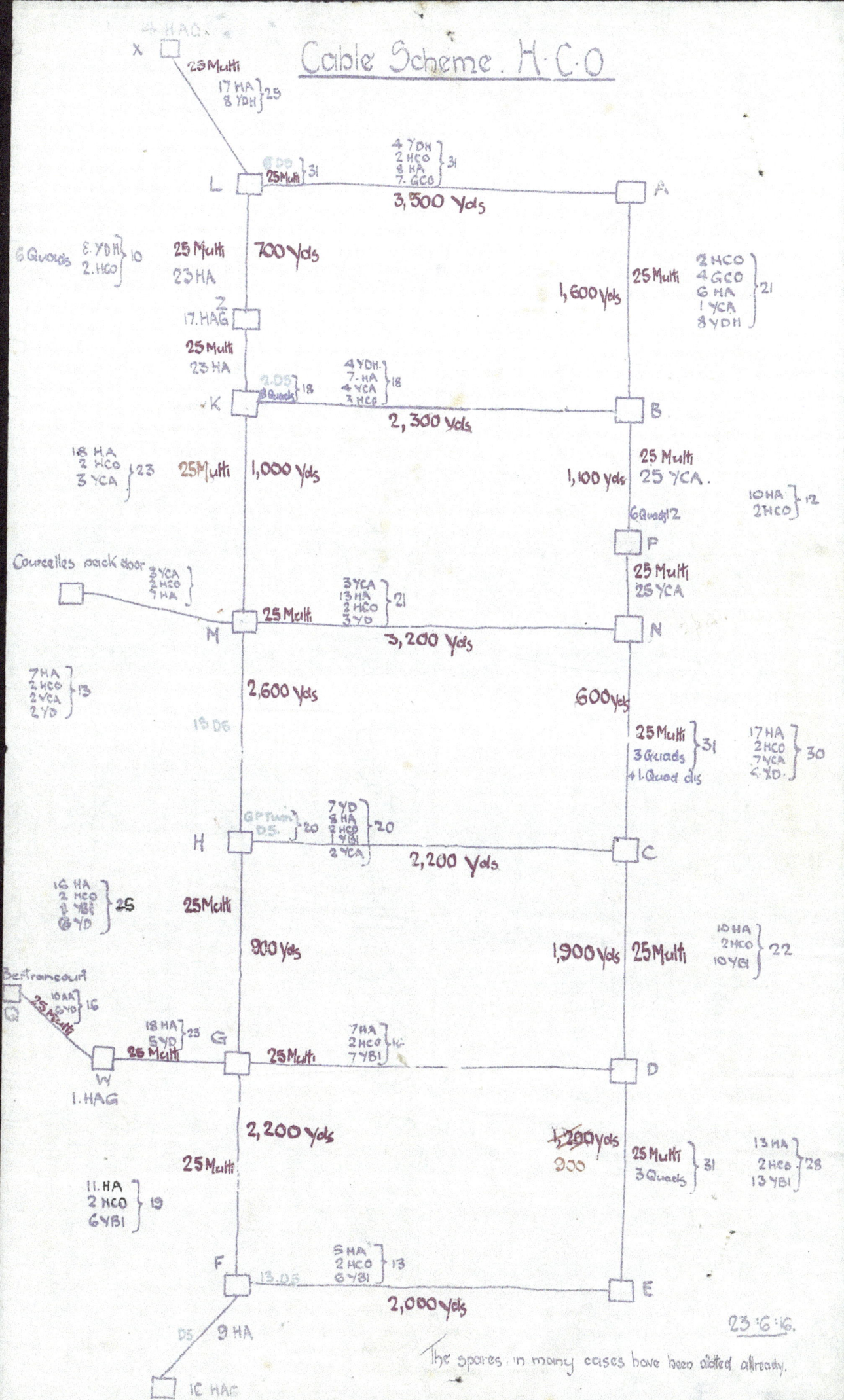

Confidential. Vol. VII 5

WAR DIARY.

31 Divisional Signal Coy R.E.

JULY

1916

Army Form C. 2118

WAR DIARY
or
INTELLIGENCE SUMMARY

31st Division Signal Coy R.E.

JULY 1916

(Erase heading not required.)

Instructions regarding War Diaries and Intelligence Summaries are contained in F. S. Regs., Part II. and the Staff Manual respectively. Title Pages will be prepared in manuscript.

Place	Date	Hour	Summary of Events and Information	Remarks and references to Appendices
BUS	JULY 1st	7.30 am	Assault commenced. All telegraph and telephone lines correct. Kept all traffic by telephone. No information or messages received by pigeon or visual. Telephone and telegraph wires stood intact throughout. Wireless not used as Bde Hq did not move forward. Runners were invaluable. For details see Appendix 7pm	A/ps 7pm
"	JULY 2nd to 4th		Normal working on buried cables	
RIBEAUCOURT	" 6th	10 am	Closed office at BUS opens at RIBEAUCOURT. All traffic disposed of by Despatch Rider.	
"	" 7th		Opens telephone to 92nd Bde at BARNAVILLE Wires via 10 Line Exchange to 8th Corps and 94th Infantry Bde.	
"	" 8th		Receive orders to entrain to join 11th Corps.	
ST VENANT	" 9th	2 pm	Closed office at RIBEAUCOURT opens at ST VENANT.	
		11.30 pm	Through morse and phone to 11th Corps 6.30 pm. Through morse to 92nd 93rd 94th Infantry Bde	
"	" 10th		Telephone and morse to each Infantry Bde, 9 Office, ASC and CRA. All wires read pretty, having been maintained by 1st Army.	

Army Form C. 2118

WAR DIARY
or
INTELLIGENCE SUMMARY
(Erase heading not required.)

Instructions regarding War Diaries and Intelligence Summaries are contained in F. S. Regs., Part II. and the Staff Manual respectively. Title Pages will be prepared in manuscript.

Place	Date	Hour	Summary of Events and Information	Remarks and references to Appendices
ST VENANT	11th		Commenced class in buzzing and telephone work for R.A. Brigade	
	12th, 13th, 14th		Routine work.	
	15th	2 pm	Closed at ST VENANT and opened new H.Q. at LESTREM. All wires led into office and labeled but no diagram. Through phone and morse to 11th Corps.	
LESTREM		4 pm	Through to 92nd Bde phone and morse.	
	16th	9 am	Laid wire to 93rd Bde also from C.R.A. to 169 7 A.B.	
	17th, 18th, 19th		All normal circuits working for the telephone and telegraph.	
	24th		Readjustment of divisional front. Our left Bn went about 400 yds right of NEUVE CHAPELLE. Took over lines from 7.39 8th Division. Becoming our new right.	
	27th		Opened an advance Telephone Exchange at VIEILLE CHAPELLE. Transferring it from FOSSE divisional Artillery H.Q.	
	28th		Germans raided our left sector all wires forward of Batty cut.	
	29th, 30th, 31st		Routine work.	
			Appendix 7 shows brief account of communication arrangements made for offensive operations	App 8 ¼

B1 Signal C5

COMMUNICATIONS.
GENERAL.

THROUGHOUT THE OPERATION.

All telegraph and telephone lines will be reserved exclusively for tactical requirements. All other messages and correspondence will be disposed of by despatch rider and orderley as opportunity occurs.

All cables are buried in trenches 6' deep in conjunction with 8th Corps Buried Cable Scheme (from a point 5500 yards behind the fron line) consisting of a series of main "Trunks" with small spurs dug off these to the various H. Q.

The scheme provides for all Infantry and Artillery circuits.

All circuits are metallic and pass through dugouts for the purpose of testing etc at the junction of each of the main trenches.

For the purpose of communications operations may be considered to be in three phases.

(1) Bombardment

(2) Assault

(3) Holding and consolidating objective.

Appendix 6.

BOMBARDMENT. (Telephone and Telegraph).

Communications will be supplemented by Despatch Rider, Runners, Visual, Pigeon and Wireless.

Separate telephone and telegraph lines are provided to each Infantry Brigade H.Q. also to Divisional O.P's.

The telephones being of the "Bell ringing" type connected to an exchange at Divisional H.Q. thus providing lateral Brigade communication.

On this exchange are also lines to Flank Divisions, Corps etc.

For list of subscribers see Appendix 1.

In addition telegraph by "Sounder" is provided direct to each Infantry Brigade H.Q. and Corps H.Q. and by "Buzzer" to each Divisional O.P.

A separate bell ringing telephone exchange is established at COURCELLES with direct lines to each Artillery Brigade H.Q. the C.R.A. and exchange at Divisional H.Q., and VIII Corps Heavies.

There will be no telegraph to Artillery Brigades but D 3 telephones will be in readiness in the event of Bell ringing telephones breaking down.

For subscribers in Artillery Exchange see Appendix 2.

Communication between Infantry Brigades and Artillery

Brigades will be via COURCELLES and D.H.Q., Exchanges.

In addition to above a buzzer exchange will be placed at H.Q., 170th Artillery Brigade having connected to it each Brigade H.Q. and Brigade O.P. and the Flank groups of the 4th & 48th Divisions. Thus providing lateral Brigade and Brigade O.P. communication.

ASSAULT.

The Artillery Group H.Q. will not be moving so their communication will be similar to previously described.

Infantry Brigade H.Q., first move from "Battle H.Q." to dugouts in SAP A and SAP D to which wires have been extended from their former H.Q.

Throughout the ASSAULT, forward of Infantry Brigade H.Q. telephone wires will probably be unreliable, but each Battalion H.Q. will run out three separate D 1 wires 20 yards apart and each man laying the wire will carry a D 3 telephone, the object of this being to establish a main Central Signal Office at Southern Edge of SERRE, K 30 c 60 55

For the purpose, in addition to telephone lines, each Brigade will arrange to send 3 separate equipped Visual Sending Stations by separate routes to the point. Pigeons and wireless (if available) will also be sent to the same place.

CONSOLIDATION OF OBJECTIVE.

Wires will be laid as soon as possible at the Southern Edge of SERRE at which a Signal Office will be opened, and the normal telegraph system will then be gradually built up.

[signed] A.F. Mair Capt.
31st Div Signal Coy

VISUAL.

Close to each of the Divisional O.P's will be a Visual Station to read messages sent from front to rear. This station will be connected direct by wire to Divisional H. Q. Units moving forward will carry discs and send each message three times over. The reading station will not answer, but read every message they see being sent.

50% of Battalion Signallers will be kept in Reserve with Battalion 1st line transport to replace casualties.

R U N N E R S.

Officers Commanding Brigade Signal Sections will make necessary arrangements for Runners with their Brigades.

During the assault at least two must be left at any H.Q., vacated. These men must know to where the H.Q., has moved. Throughout the operations each Infantry and Artillery Brigade H.Q., will send two permanent Orderlies (Cyclists) to ColinCamps Signal Office for communication to and from their Units.

These men will be under orders of O.C. Divisional Signal Coy

PIGEON SERVICE.

Pigeons are available, and will be alloted as follows:-

        To 94th Bde   16.

        To 93rd Bde.   16.

        To 94th Bde.   14.

They will not be taken in advance of Battalion H.Q., and will be allotted to Battalions carrying out the Brown, Blue and Red bounds under orders of Brigade Signalling Officers, who will ensure that each man carrying pigeon is supplemented by a second man following the first at 20 or 30 yards distance.

They must not be liberated during the dark, and should be used for emergency only.

These birds are trained to return to loft at Divisional H.Q.

W I R E L E S S.

If available, two trench sets capable of working over a distance of not more than 4,000 yards will be installed.

A SET at the S.W. edge of SERRE.

B SET at H.Q. 170th F.A.B.

B SET will be connected by wire to Divisional Headquarters. and also worked to a "Wilson" set farther West in conjunction with Signals VIII Corps.

It is essential to remember than any message sent by wireless can be "tapped" by the enemy and also that delivery of messages thus transmitted is slow.

APPENDIX 1.

Subscribers to BUS Exchange (50 Lines)

- (1) G. Office.
- (2) G. Office.
- (3) C. R. A.
- (4) C. R. A.
- (5) A. A. & Q.
- (6) Signals.
- (7) VIII Corps.
- (8) Corps Heavy Artillery
- (9) 48th Division
- (10) 4th Division
- (11) 92nd Inf Bde
- (12) 93rd Inf Bde
- (13) 94th Inf Bde
- (14) North Divisional O.P.
- (15) South Divisional O.P.
- (16) COURCELLES Exchange
- (17) COURCELLES Exchange
- (18) A.D.M.S.
- (19) Divisional Train.

APPENDIX 2

Subscribers to Artillery Exchange.

(1) C.R.A.

(2) BUS Exchange

(3) BUS Exchange

(4) 165th F. A. B.

(5) 169th F. A. B.

(6) 170th F. A. B.

(7) 171st F. A. B.

BRIEF REPORT ON COMMUNICATIONS DURING OPERATIONS ON JULY 1st 1916.

All telegraph and telephone circuits throughout the Division worked excellently all through the weeks bombardment and during the assault.

ASSAULT. (GENERAL).

First information was obtained verbally by phone from Divisional O.P.

All through the day of assault "1st July" the greatest part of traffic was on the telephone.

ARTILLERY.

At first only Bell Phone was allowed for, but during bombardment telegraph had to be opened up as it was found that the telephone lines were apt to be congested by transmitting telegrams over them. The telegrams being chiefly Ordnance, indents for spare gun parts and also casualty and ammunition returns.

VISUAL.

There was never much opportunity to use this, but both Artillery and Staff from their O.P's, gained much information as to position of troops from tin discs sewn on the mens backs reflecting the sun.

WIRELESS.

Not required during bombardment as all lines stood, and there was no opportunity of using it during the assault.

PIGEON.

Our troops never got really sufficiently forward for them to be made use of.

RUNNERS.

These were invaluable.

Confidential   Vol VII
Vol 6

War Diary
of
3rd Div: Signal Coy

August 1916.

Army Form C. 2118

WAR DIARY or INTELLIGENCE SUMMARY

(Erase heading not required.)

31st DIVISIONAL SIGNAL COY. R.E.

AUGUST 1916

Place	Date	Hour	Summary of Events and Information	Remarks and references to Appendices
LESTREM	AUG 1st to 3rd		Normal routine work. Appendix 8 shows diagram of communications on Aug 1st.	App 8
	4th 5th 6th		Building route for 170 Bty R.G.A to their battery.	
	7th 8th 9th		Normal routine work.	
			Building separate "Buzzer" route for emergency on all lines run at present. Same pole line. To be worked by means of a buzzer exchange at VIEILLE CHAPELLE.	
	10th		Temporary readjustment of divisional front. 92nd bde moving from divisional reserve to take over the FESTUBERT section and 89th Bde becoming divisional reserve at VIEILLE CHAPELLE. Communication obtained both telegraph and telephone via 92nd Bde. "C" Group R.A. at LOISNE came under 81st R.A. Control - telephone via 92nd Bde at Cse du RAUX.	
	11th to 17th 18th		Routine work. Nothing of special interest to bring to notice.	
			Handed over NEUVE CHAPELLE sector to 183rd Bde 61st division. The 94th going into divisional reserve at VIEILLE CHAPELLE.	
	19th to 25th		Normal routine work. 8 buried pairs of wires found during this period. Failed to record seemed to exist. On 24th had first news of a proposed attack by 2 brigades in front	

Army Form C. 2118

WAR DIARY
or
INTELLIGENCE SUMMARY
(Erase heading not required.)

Instructions regarding War Diaries and Intelligence Summaries are contained in F.S. Regs., Part II. and the Staff Manual respectively. Title Pages will be prepared in manuscript.

Place	Date	Hour	Summary of Events and Information	Remarks and references to Appendices
LESTREM.	August 26 to 29th		of about 1500 yds. Everything to be ready by September 6th. 9th Bde from VIEILLE CHAPELLE to 8 MAISONS.	
	29th		Routine work, mainly replacing stays, which have been badly damaged by farmers cutting corn and ploughing. On nearly all "Comic" routes stays were taken up and not replaced.	
	30th to 31st		Routine work.	
			No alterations to main routes during the month. Appendix 9 shows "Traffic" record for the month of telegraph and registered sealed packets.	App 9.

J. A. F. Shaw Capt.
31st Div. Signal Coy.

Appendix 8.

COMMUNICATIONS 31ST DIV LESTREM.

Local Circuits
- GOC
- G
- A&Q
- Signals
- ADMS
- DAPOS
- CRE
- APM

Red ——— Bell Phone
Blue ═══ Buzzer on Telegraph

1st 8:16

Appendix 9

TRAFFIC RECORD

August : 1916

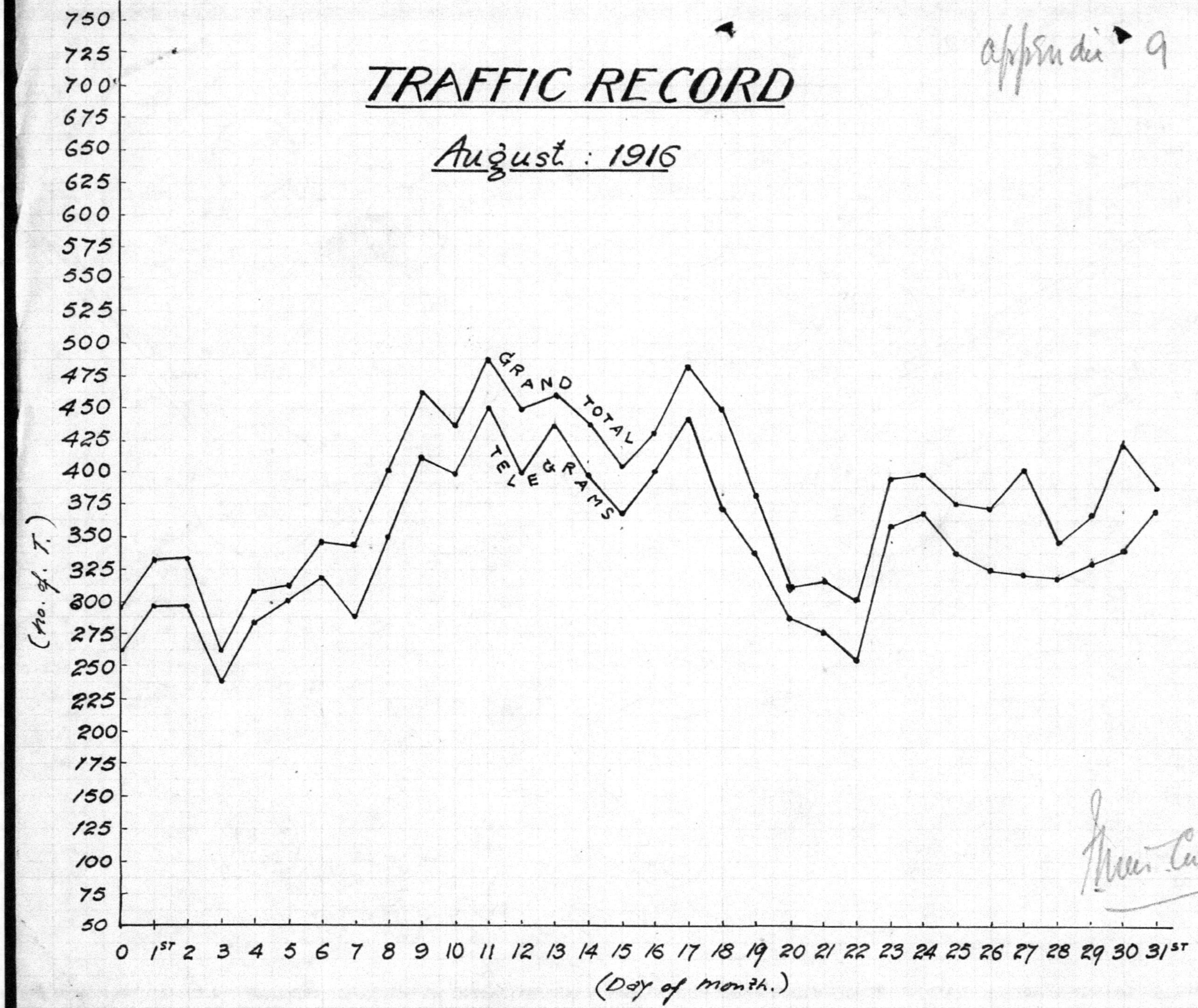

Confidential

Vol XY

War Diary.

31st Divisional Signal Coy. Royal Engineers

September 1916

Army Form C. 2118

WAR DIARY
or
INTELLIGENCE SUMMARY
(Erase heading not required.)

RE 31st DIVISION SIGNAL COMPANY

Place	Date Sept	Hour	Summary of Events and Information	Remarks and references to Appendices
LESTREM	1st		SEPTEMBER Rear Battery positions for offensive definitely notified in the evening up to this time unable to commence on their communication not knowing positions.	
"	2nd		Laid a ditched twisted D/3 from 92nd Battle HQ to 92nd new Battle HQ.	
"	3rd		93rd Brigade withdrawn from FESTUBERT SECTOR and moved to DIV reserve at VIEILLE CHAPELLE FESTUBERT SECTOR handed over to the 30th DIV	
"	4th		Opened telegraph to MERVILLE open lift	
"	5th		Laid a ditched cable D/3 from 8 MAISONS to 94th Battle HQ.	
"	6th		Communication ready for proposed offensive with exception RA OP lines which will not be laid until the batteries move into positions. App 10 a + b above arrangements made	App 10 a + b
"	7th		Routine work	
"	8th		Commenced Comic "H" route from 94th Battle HQ at ST VAAST to their Peace WR at 8 MAISONS.	
"	9th		Routine work	
"	10th		Normal	
"	15th		Received orders 39 DIV HQ to move to LOCON on 18th taking over the FESTUBERT and GIVENCHY sectors from 30th DIV.	
"	16th		All wires advanced 24 hours. Opened Telegraph to LOCON and began to man the place as a Forward Report Centre	
"	17th		At 11.30 am had all 3 Infantry Brigades working through LOCON both Telegraph and Telephone also Corps and Flank Divisions. 12 wires opened HQ at LOCON. The CRA remaining at FOSSE and Group HQ not moving until 18th No difficulty experienced in picking up the circuits from LOCON to the Brigades owing to ample supply of diagrams and labelling	

WAR DIARY
or
INTELLIGENCE SUMMARY

(Erase heading not required.)

Army Form C. 2118

Place	Date	Hour	Summary of Events and Information	Remarks and references to Appendices
LOCON	18th		Div Artillery Head Quarters moved from FOSSE to new Headquarters about 3/4 mile West of LOCON, necessitating laying of fresh lines which would have been previously had Locon been heavily shelled. This was impossible owing to the former Artillery Headquarters at LOCON being occupied by Divisional Headquarters.	
"	19th		Fresh Artillery Exchange at old Artillery HQrs Locon, connecting it to Group HQs, Heavies and divisional exchange. Very heavy rain. Comic lines damaged by rain of 18th owing to steep banks up to far mess. Work normal.	
	20th to 25th		Reeling up wire. The XI Corps bending a cable nearer. Establishing signalling buzzers along the Rue de Bois.	
	26th to 29th		Routine work.	
	30th		First intimation of move to 1st Army Area. 5th Division Established at LESTREM. Appendix 11 shows traffic return for the month.	App. 11.

J. A. T. Marsden Capt.
3' Div Signal Coy.

App 10 A

Telegraph
Buzzer Telegraph
Bell Phone for RA
Staff & General.

APP-10B

Legend:
Telegraph
Buzzer Telegraph
Bell Phone for RA
Staff & General.

- BATTLE HQ & LEFT GROUP X
- BATTLE HQ 92 & RIGHT GROUP X
- TO FLANK BDE
- CSE DU RAUX
- 3 MAISONS & CRA
- VIS VIEILLE CHAPELLE
- RES. BDE
- CRA
- X20 LESTREM

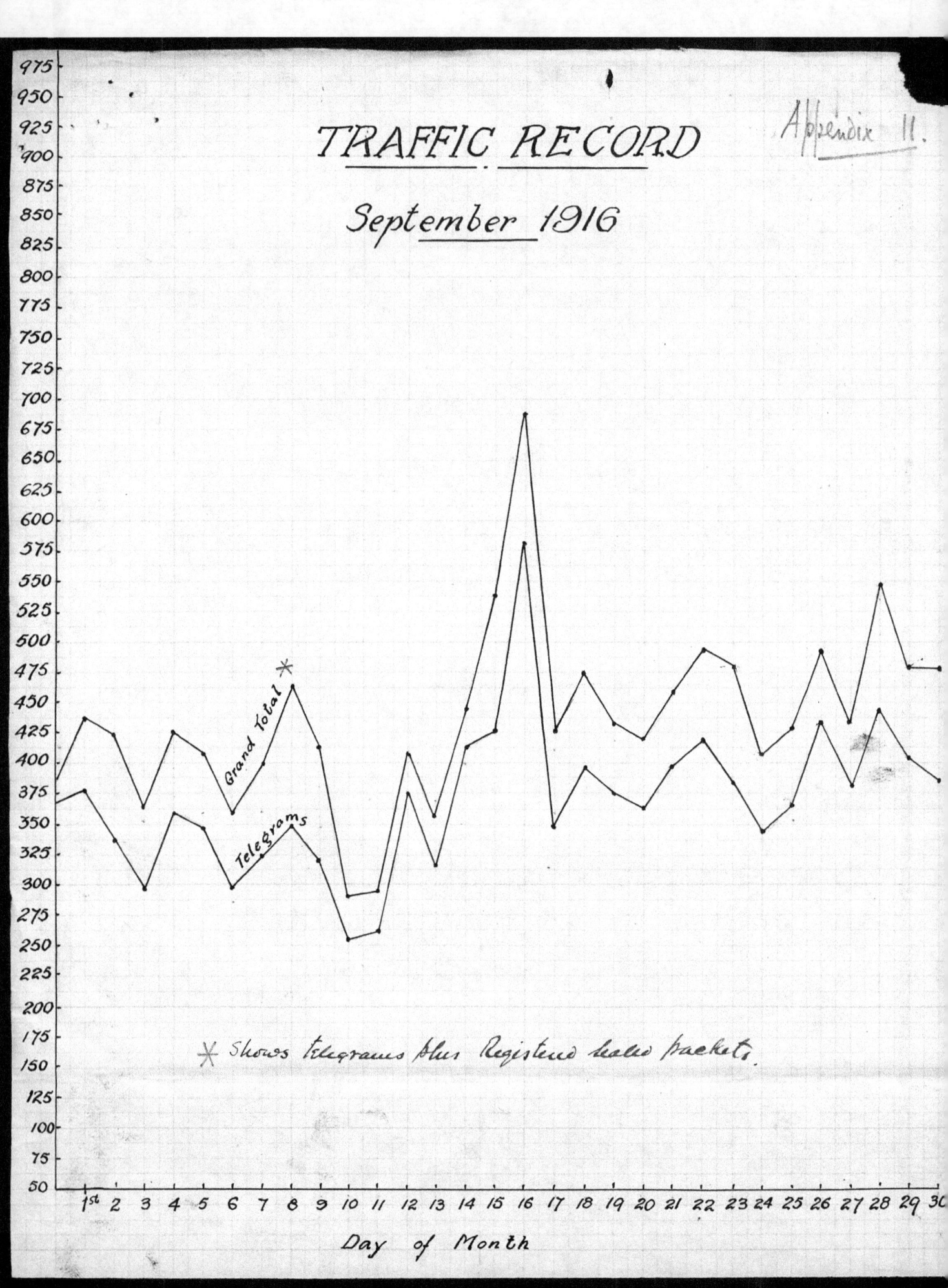

Confidential

Volume X
Vol 8

War Diary.
31st Divisional Signal Coy R.E.

October 1916.

Army Form C. 2118

WAR DIARY
or
INTELLIGENCE SUMMARY

(Erase heading not required.)   31st DIV SIGNAL COY R.E.

Place	Date	Hour	Summary of Events and Information	Remarks and references to Appendices
LOCON	October 1915		Preparing to move over-hauling stores etc	
"	2nd		- ditto -	
"	3rd		Commenced handing over to 5th Div Signals.	
	4th		- do -	
	5th		Infantry Brigades moved to MERVILLE, BUSNES and ROBECQ managers to the two latter places being delivered by D.R. and MERVILLE via XI Corps Telegraph. G.O.C. 5th Div assumed command of the front.	
	6 R.		Composite divisional artillery relieved 31st Div artillery.	
	7th			
	8 R.	7.20 am	Entrained MERVILLE detraining at CANDAS marching to MARIEUX where div. H.Q opened at 10 a.m. Came into XIII Corps.	
MARIEUX	9 R.		Opened telegraph to Infantry brigades at VAUCHELLES THIEVES and SARTON. Two Artillery Brigades being attached to 19th div and the other 6.5.T.5.M for an offensive of XI Corps. The 31st division being in corps reserve.	
	10 R.		All Officers and Linesmen learning the 19th and 57th areas with the possibility of taking over their front & then during or after the offensive.	
	11 R.		- ditto -	
	12 R.			

WAR DIARY
or
INTELLIGENCE SUMMARY
(Erase heading not required.)

Army Form C. 2118

Place	Date	Hour	Summary of Events and Information	Remarks and references to Appendices
MARIEUX	13th		Oct (cont^d)	
	15th		Date of Offensive postponed from 18th to 20th Oct.	
	16th		Orders to take over the line from 19th Div. 92nd Bde to take over the front and remained under orders of 19th Div.	
AUTHIE	17th		Div. HQ moved to AUTHIE and took command of the line. The majority of forward circuits on forced routes 6' deep. 92nd Bde HQ firing at SAILLY QUARRIES. Communication by telephone established to infantry and artillery by forward exchange at SAILLY QUARRIES, a meeting point for nearly all wires.	
	19th		Routine work.	
	20th		A 5 line rapid exchange installed at RELIANCE CORNER into the 3 field companies connected to it.	
	21st		93rd Bde relieved the 92nd. CRA 31 Div. moved his Headquarters to SAILLY QUARRIES.	
	22nd		Commenced to prepare for an attack by 92nd Bde with 2 batt alive with div. HQ remaining at AUTHIE.	
	23rd		For the offensive advanced Div HQ was to have been opened at SAILLY QUARRIES.	

WAR DIARY
or
INTELLIGENCE SUMMARY

Army Form C. 2118

(Erase heading not required.)

Place	Date	Hour	Summary of Events and Information	Remarks and references to Appendices
AUTHIE	Oct (cont) 24th		Making arrangements for advanced HQ at SAILLY. Date of attack postponed for 24 hours. Advanced divisional HQ at SAILLY cancelled and decided on at place near CONGREVE when we were billeted. Date of attack postponed a further 48 hours.	
			Appendix 12 details of arrangements for communication to attack See App.12. Appendix 13 gives diagram of communication to attack with advanced HQ at SAILLY. SAILLY QUARRIES shelled and majority of circuits cut.	App 12 App 13
	25th		Reserve army signals built airline 20 line route to Battle HQ from Regt of 350 yards.	
	26th		Wiring and working at Battle HQ. Installing a 20 line telephone exchange	
	27th		— ditto — offensive postponed a further 48 hours	
	28th		Battle HQ to be looking ready. Weather very wet further 48 hours postponement.	
	29th 30th		Normal work	
	31st		Date of offensive fixed for 5th November. The greater majority of both artillery and infantry lines on forced routes but most of very bad being buried cables taken up. Appendix 14 shows diagram of traffic for the month. 31st Oct Major Thompson 31st Oct Dr Deyester	

S E C R E T.   COPY NO. ....

APPENDIX. 12

SUPPLEMENTARY INSTRUCTIONS 'A' TO
31st DIVISION ORDER NO. 69

A. GENERAL   Throughout the operations all telegraph and telephone lines will be reserved exclusively for tactical requirements, and other messages will be disposed of by Motor Cyclist or Runner as opportunities occur.

B. TELEGRAPH & TELEPHONE.

All cables forward of a line N & S through SAILLY and COURCELLES are buried 6 feet deep.

A 20 line Exchange is installed both at AUTHIE and SAILLY and a 10 line Artillery Exchange. Subscribers on these are as follows :-

AUTHIE EXCHANGE.		SAILLY EXCHANGE.		R.A. EXCHANGE.	
SAILLY Ex.	2 lines.	XIII Corps	2 lines	SAILLY Ex.	2 lines
"G"	1 "	AUTHIE Ex.	2 "	3rd. Div.) Arty.)	1 "
"Q"	1 "	"G"	2 "		
C.R.E.	1 "	33rd Div.) Arty.)	1 "	31 Div.) Arty.)	2 "
R.E. Ex.	1 "	92nd Bde.	2 "		
94th Bde.	1 "	93rd Bde.	1 "	33 Div.) Arty.)	1 "
Div. Train	1 "	3rd Div.	1 "		
A.P.M.	1 "	49th Div.	1 "	165 F.A.B.	1 "
D.A.D.O.S.	1 "	144 Bde.	1 "	169 "	1 "
Signals	1 "	42 H.A.G.	1 "	170 "	1 "
Corps) Hospital)	1 "	Signals	1 "	D.T.M.O.	1 "
		COURCELLES) Ex.)	1 "		
		R.A. Ex.	2 "		

In addition to above 31 Div. "G" have private line to XIII Corps "G" and 33rd Div. R.A. and 3rd R.A. have private lines to XIIIth Corps R.A.

There is direct telegraph from Advanced Divisional Headquarters at SAILLY QUARRIES to the following :-

(a) XIII Corps
(b) 92nd Brigade
(c) AUTHIE & 94th Brigade.
(d) Pigeon Loft.
(e) 3rd Div. BUS.
(f) and via 92nd Brigade for :-

    2 Bns. 12th & 13th E.Yorks. at K.23.c.35.60
        (junction of WRANGLE & CABER)

    1 Bn. 11th E.Yorks. K.22.d.05.6. (near junction
        of JEAN BART and GUESCLIN)

    1 Bn. 10th E.Yorks. K.22.c.37. (near junction
        of VERCINGETORIX and HOME).

From K.21 Central buried routes are carried forward down HOME Trench to the junction of CABER and WRANGLE whence they separate to K.23.c.26 and K.23.d.12. The former serving as a jumping off place for Battalions to extend lines from.

'C' PIGEON SERVICE.

Pigeons will be delivered by XIII Corps to SANDY QUARRIES whence they will be forwarded by 31st Division in Stock baskets to 92nd. Infantry Brigade., at K.21 central. Brigade Pigeon men will take them forward from there in Trench baskets to Battalion H.Q. where not less than two will be given to each Company H.Q.

Messages will be telegraphed from the lofts to the addressees, all messages being treated as "PRIORITY".

The following will be the allotment :-

At Brigade H.Q. reserve of 12.
To 12th. E. York R. 12.
To 13th. E. York R. 12.

Small baskets carrying 2 pigeons each will be used for Battalion and Company pigeons.

The birds must only be liberated in DAYLIGHT and NOT IF MISTY.

'D' VISUAL.

A Battalion visual reading station will be established at K.23.c.28 (the junction of JUNGLE and C.B.R) and a Brigade station at K.21 Central.

These stations will read messages sent from front to rear. Any visual message being sent will be sent as follows :-

Each word repeated and each message sent twice.

One French Lamp will be allotted to each Btn.H.Q. and one at Bde.H.Q. and can be used either for visual or for communicating to Aeroplanes.

Signallers sending messages back must be instructed to send in a general direction towards the PYEON ridge to a point about 1000 yards South of HEBUTERNE.

'E' RUNNERS.

Will wear blue armlet with WHITE Band.
The following is the scale per Brigade :-
At Bde. H.Q. 20.
At Bn. H.Q. 12.
Coy. H.Q. 4.

O i/c Signals 92nd. Bde. will arrange details of relay posts etc. forward of Bde. H.Q.

'F' PERSONNEL.

50% of Battalion Signallers will be left with Brigade Transport to form reinforcements. They will be under control of Brigade Section Signal Officer.

W. B. Spender.
Lieut-Colonel
General Staff.

Copy No.1	Div. R.A.	Copy No.11	Office Copy.
2	Div. R.E.	12)	War Diary.
3	92 Inf. Bde.	13)	
4	93 " "	14	3rd. Division.
5	94 " "	15	49th. Division.
6	Div. Pioneers.	16	XIII Corps 'G'
7	Div. Signal Coy.	17	" " 'Q'
8	A.D.M.S.	18	O.C.2nd.M.G.Squad
9	S.A.	19	1st.Ind.Cav.Div.
10	A.P.M.	20	O.C.No.1 Special Coy R.E.

Copy No.20. D.Coy.No.1 Special Coy R.E.
" " 21 5th. Squad. R.F.Corps.
" " 22 O.C. C.Coy. Heavy Section M.G. Coy.

COMMUNICATIONS 31st DIVn.

— SAILLY QUARRIES occupied as advanced Divl. H.Q.

APPENDIX 13

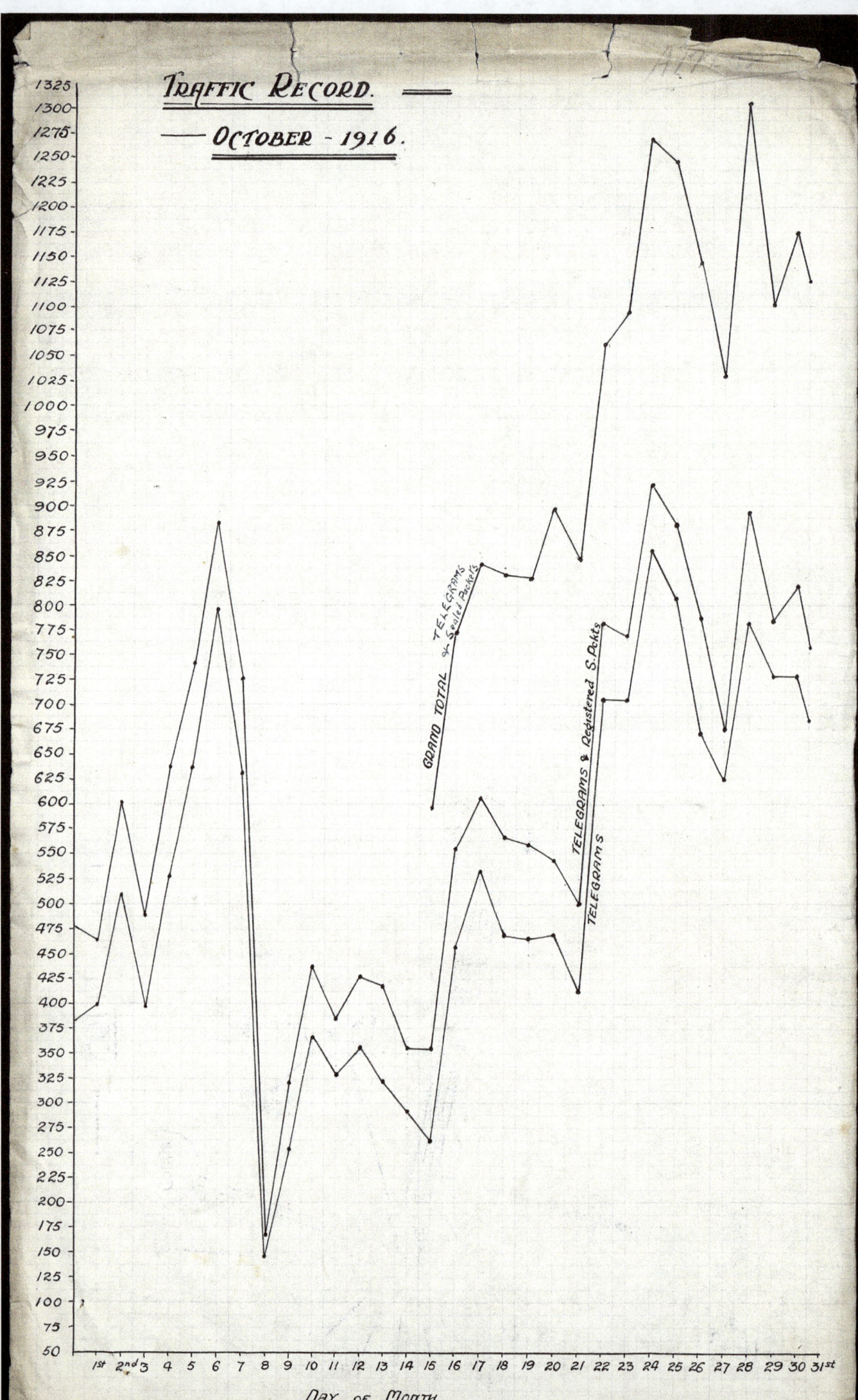

Confidential

Volume XI

Vol 9

War Diary.

31st Divisional Signal Coy. R.E.

November 1916.

WAR DIARY or INTELLIGENCE SUMMARY

Army Form C. 2118

Place: AUTHIE
[Unit]: 31st Divl. Signal Coy. R.E.
[Month]: November 1916

Date	Hour	Summary of Events and Information	Remarks and references to Appendices
Nov. 1st		Working on forward buried routes put down by former division but not completed.	
2nd		Working on buried routes.	
3rd		— ditto —	
4th		93rd Bde. H.Q. moved from SAILLY to advanced divisional H.Q. near COIGNEAU. Routine work. Date of offensive indefinitely postponed.	
5th		Routine work. Corps took over all buried cable routes, maintenance etc.	
6th		Routine work. Presence of 1 officer (2nd Lt. P.S. Bagley) 1 Corporal and 12 men.	
7th		Very wet. 93rd Bde relieved 94th. Routine work.	
8th		Normal work.	
9th		— do —	
10th		— do —	
11th		— do —	
12th 10pm		Officers advanced divisional H.Q. at 92nd & 93rd Bde. H.Q. moved to their advanced H.Q.	
13th		92nd Bde attacked with two battalions. All lines held throughout the operations except to the right division which was out of communication for about 2 hours. Their lines being broken about 200 yds from their advanced H.Q. The 92nd Bde has were working to our front line throughout the day but although twenty five attempts were made to get through across to the German front line, "no mans land".	

Army Form C. 2118

WAR DIARY
or
INTELLIGENCE SUMMARY
(Erase heading not required.)

Instructions regarding War Diaries and Intelligence Summaries are contained in F. S. Regs., Part II. and the Staff Manual respectively. Title Pages will be prepared in manuscript.

Place	Date	Hour	Summary of Events and Information	Remarks and references to Appendices
AUTHIE	Nov		cont?	
	14th		They were unsuccessful. The wires being broken or the prisoners being killed or wounded. No visual messages by heliograph or aeroplane contact patrol work possible owing to a thick mist. No pigeon messages received. Very few runners were able to get through the German barrage. See Appendices	Appendix 17m
do	15th		Adv Div HQ closed 7.30 am. 92nd Batt 93rd, 94th Bde moved respectively to S: LEDGER, Adv Div HQ and SAILLY. The 94th holding the line 120 Bde of 40th div holding the 3rd BUTERN sector came temporally under orders of 31st Div	
	16th		Normal work. Tracing and laying lost buried routes	
	17th		" " " " " "	
	18th		" " " " " "	
	19th		" " " " " "	
	20th		" " " " " "	
	21st		Took over the HEBUTERN sector from 120 Bde. 3 Bdes in the line. HQ as follows 120 Bde to St LEGER	
	22nd		120 Bde left 31st Div Area. Tracing out buried routes in Hebutern Sector	
	23rd		" " " " " "	
	24th		" " " " " "	

Army Form C. 2118

WAR DIARY
or
INTELLIGENCE SUMMARY
(Erase heading not required.)

Instructions regarding War Diaries and Intelligence Summaries are contained in F.S. Regs., Part II. and the Staff Manual respectively. Title Pages will be prepared in manuscript.

Place	Date	Hour	Summary of Events and Information	Remarks and references to Appendices
AUTHIE	25th		Tracing buried routes in the Hebuterne Sector. Informed Div HQ would move to COUIN on 30th. Now opening 12 noon	
"	26th		Tracing and testing buried routes.	
"	27th		– do –	
"	28th		– do –	
"	29th		Preparing to move to COUIN.	
"	30		Opened Div HQ at COUIN at 12 noon. All circuits working normally at 1:30. 4 pm Div Artillery H.Q. moved from SAILLY QUARRIES to COUIN. Appendix 14 shows traffic during month.	App 14 2.

J.A.T. Muir Capt.
O.C. 31 Div. Signal Coy. R.E.

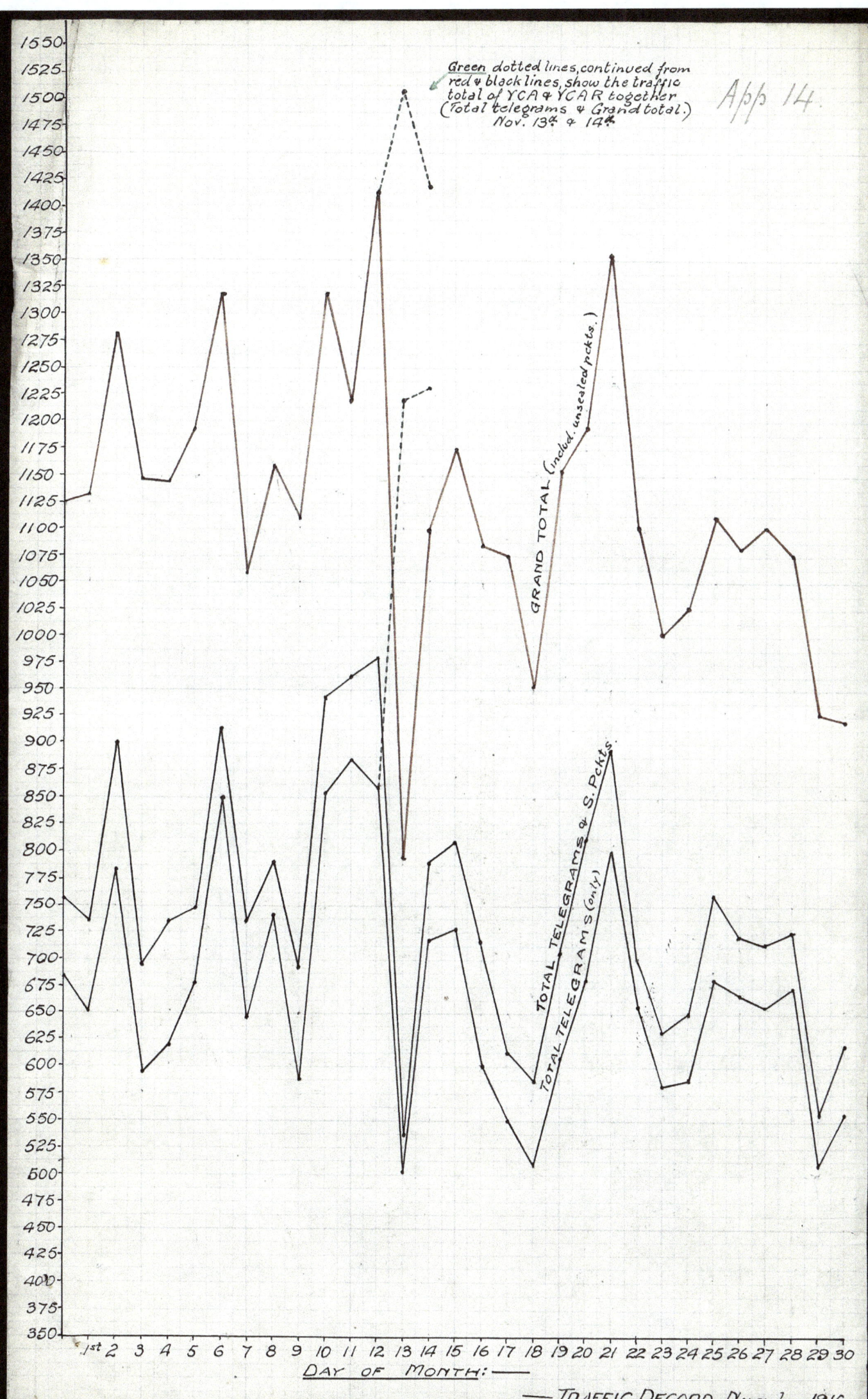

Confidential

Volume XII

Vol 10

War Diary.

31st Divisional Signal Coy R.E.

December.

Army Form C. 2118

WAR DIARY
or
INTELLIGENCE SUMMARY
(Erase heading not required.)

31st SIGNAL COY R.E.

DECEMBER 1916

Place	Date	Hour	Summary of Events and Information	Remarks and references to Appendices
COUIN	1st		Brigade "maintenance" parties increased to 1 Officer and 20 O.R. and employed on clearing cables in the trenches. Each brigade clearing its own area, commencing on Southern boundary and working North.	
"	2nd		Routine work	
"	3rd		Recovering disused cables, and testing and tracing disused buried routes.	
"	4th R		" "	
"	5th R		" "	
"	6th R		Normal work	
"	7th R		" "	
"	8th R		" "	
"	9th R		93rd Bde moved to BAYENCOURT. 92nd Bde moved to AUTHIE leaving 2 Bdes in the line	
"	10th R		Normal work	
"	11th R		Tracing buried routes -	
"	12th R		Tracing and testing buried routes	
"	13th R		Normal work. Tracing and testing buried routes	
"	14th R		" "	
"	15th R		" "	
"	16th R		" "	
"	17th R		" "	

WAR DIARY or INTELLIGENCE SUMMARY

Army Form C. 2118

Place	Date	Hour	Summary of Events and Information	Remarks and references to Appendices
COUIN	18th		Renovating old buried routes.	
"	19th		" "	
"	20th		Siting new cable trench round eastern edge of HEBUTERNE with a view to its taking in "OP's" for both Heavy and Field Artillery.	
"	21st		Tried out the trench both ways. The cable trench to be dug 8 foot deep and to be completed by 1st January. This date being fixed by XIII Corps. Too intricate, and 1 station R.E. allotted for the work.	
"	22nd		Telephone Exchange broke down for about 1 hour owing to ringing and speaking circuits short-circuiting.	
"	23rd		Commenced to dig cable trench. Very windy with rain. Digging in two sectors.	
"	24th		Digging cable trench.	
"	25th		Holiday as far as possible.	
"	26th		Digging HEBUTERNE cable trench	
"	27th		Laying cables (40 pairs) in cable trench.	
"	28th		Commenced second sector of cable trench	
"	29th		Digging cable trench	
"	30th		Finished excavating and laying cables	
"	31st		Filling in cable trench. Cadet under Mr WHITTAKER at BEAUQUESNE Signal School under 1st Course 30 strong, of Divisional Signallers.	

APPENDIX 16 gives diagram of traffic for month of December.

[signature] O.C. No. 3 Coy. 31.12.16. App/16.

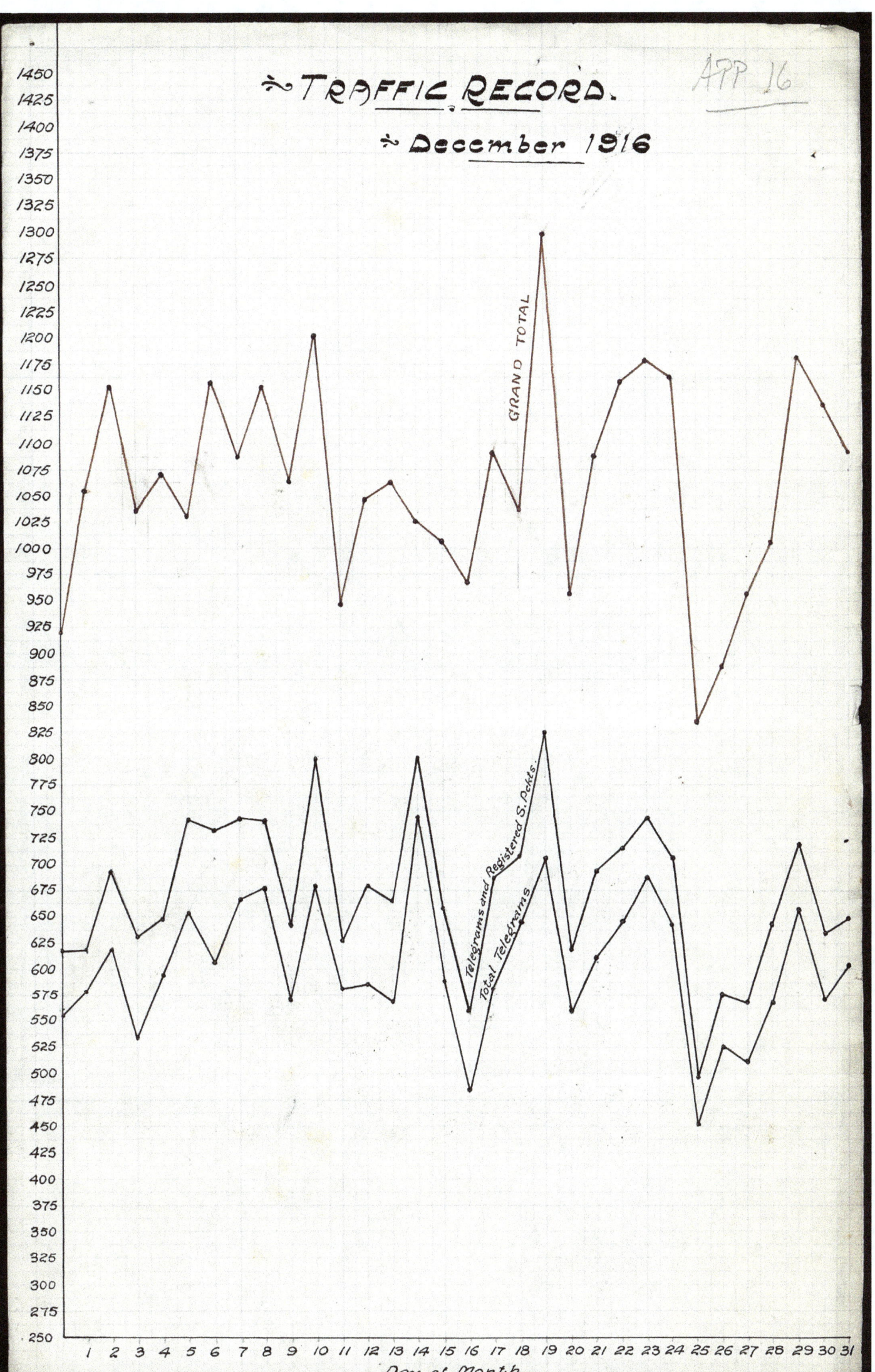

Confidential

Volume XIII

Vol XI

War Diary.

31st Divisional Signal Company. R.E.

January 1917.

WAR DIARY
or
INTELLIGENCE SUMMARY

Army Form C. 2118

(Erase heading not required.)

31 Signal Coy R.E.

Place	Date	Hour	Summary of Events and Information	Remarks and references to Appendices
COVIN	Jan/1917 1st		Routine work - filling in Hebuterne cable trench	
	2nd		Reserve brigade relieve left brigade of Beaumont command at 2/pm. Testing cables in "Hebuterne Bury" & filling in trench.	
	3rd		Routine work - filling in Hebuterne cable trench & erection of test poles.	
	4th		— do —	
	5th		— do —	
	6th		Divisional Operation Orders re move of division from line to rear area with D.H.Q. at Beauval.	
	7th		Routine work - filling in Hebuterne cable trench	
	8th		— do —	
	9th		— do — Hebuterne cable trench completed	
	10th		— do — 3rd Div. on our right relieved by 32nd Div. at 11.0 a.m.	
	11th		— do — Communication from Beauval arranged 92nd Bde relieved by 5 & 6 Bde at 2-15 p.m. 92nd Bde opened at Amplier. Division H.Q. close at Couin at 12-0 p.m. & open at Beauval 12-0 noon Relieved by 19th Division. 94th Bde H.Q. relieved by 58 Bde H.Q. at 12 noon	

Army Form C. 2118

WAR DIARY
or
INTELLIGENCE SUMMARY
(Erase heading not required.)

Instructions regarding War Diaries and Intelligence Summaries are contained in F.S. Regs., Part II. and the Staff Manual respectively. Title Pages will be prepared in manuscript.

Place	Date	Hour	Summary of Events and Information	Remarks and references to Appendices
BEAUVAL	Jan 11		Army local signal office taken over by us. 5th Corps at Doullens transmitting traffic to 92nd Bde. at Ampiens and 93rd Bde at Authieule.	
	12	noon	31st Div. Artillery H.Q. at Comm relieved by 19th Div. H.Q.r	
		6pm	31st Div Artillery H.Q. open at Therves and communication obtained thro' Siege Park Exchange.	
	13	3pm	C.R.E. at Bernaville connected to Bernaville Exchange.	
	14		Routine work	
	15		Went down, 30 o.r. assembled at 31st Div. Signal School Beauvert.	
	16			
	17		Overhauling Equipment, stores etc	
	18		2/Lt SMITH. H.S. joined as supernumerary Officer	
	19		31 Div Artillery H.Q. moved to DOULLENS	
	20		Overhauling stores etc	
	21		30 O.R. en-trulled at 31 Div Signal School BEAUMETZ	

Army Form C. 2118

WAR DIARY
or
INTELLIGENCE SUMMARY

(Erase heading not required.)

31 SIGNAL COY R.E.

Place	Date	Hour	Summary of Events and Information	Remarks and references to Appendices
BERNAVILLE	22		Moved to BERNAVILLE 12 noon. 92nd Bde to GAIZENCOURT 93rd to MT PLAISIR 94th remained at BEAUVAL. Took over 5th Army Exchange at BERNAVILLE Office.	
"	23			
"	24		Mushrooming Equipment, lines etc.	
"	25			
"	26			
"	27		5th Course at Div Signal School commenced raising total number of Students up to 150.	
"	28		Brigade sections came in to BERNAVILLE before remainder of coy for training.	
"	29		92nd Bde moved to BERTEAUCOURT.	
"	30		Repairing bicycles etc.	
"	31		Appendix 17 gives traffic records for the month.	App 17

J.P. ... Capt.
R.E.
O.C. 31 Div. Signal Coy R.E.

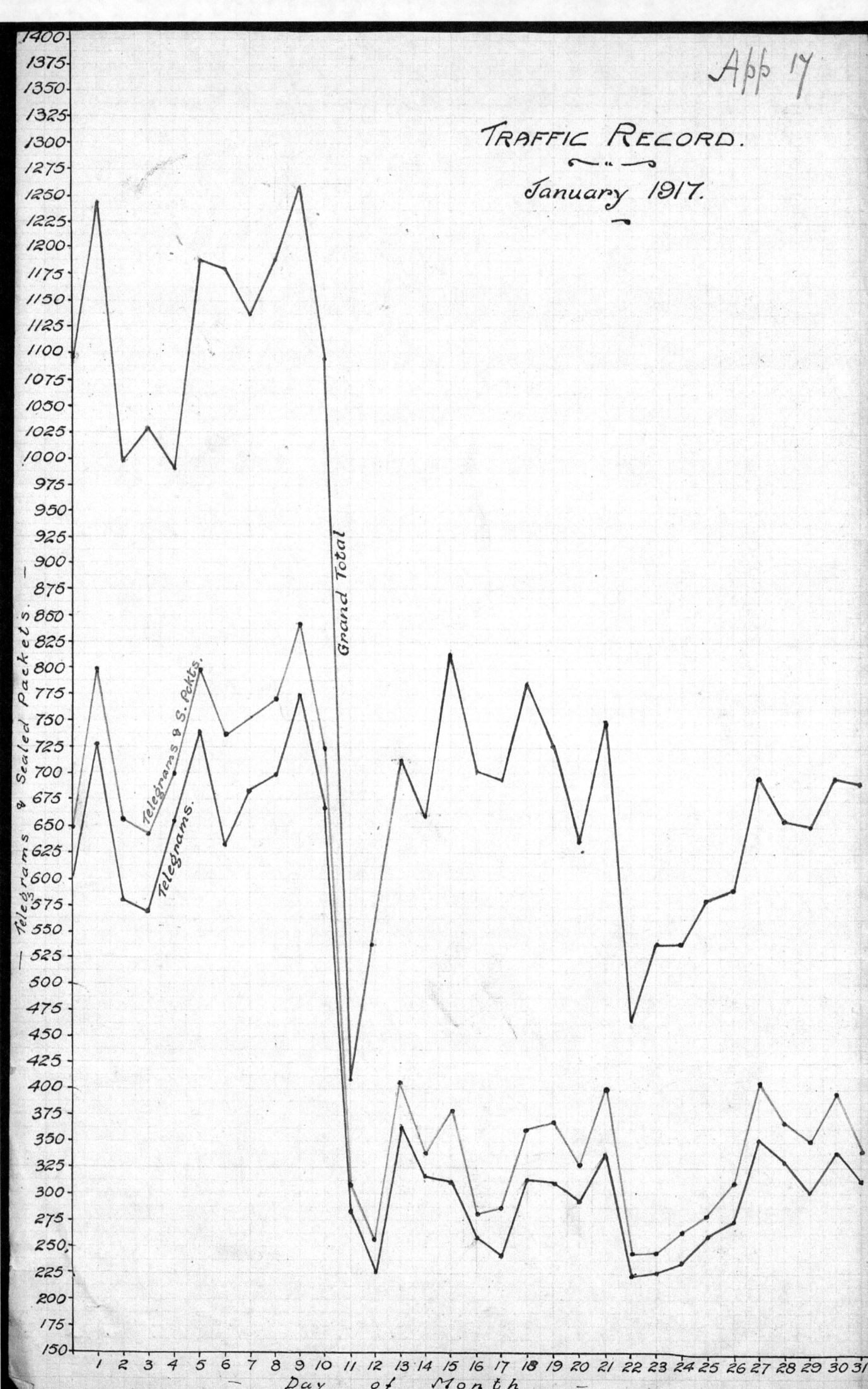

Confidential

Volume XIV

Vol 12

War Diary.

31st Divisional Signal Coy. R.E.

February 1917.

Army Form C. 2118

WAR DIARY
or
INTELLIGENCE SUMMARY
(Erase heading not required.)

FEBRUARY 1917   31 SIGNAL COY RE

Place	Date	Hour	Summary of Events and Information	Remarks and references to Appendices
BERNAVILLE	1st		Hq div A.S. and Brigade RA. DAC moved to St OUEN. Telephone exche nly available bet army exchange at DOMART to which one pair of wires had to have 92nd Bde as well.	
"	2.		Training of Coy. Store management. Cable laying - demonstration of listening apparatus.	
	3		⎫	
	4		⎬ Training coy &c - Cable laying visual	
	5		⎭	
	6		⎫	
	7		⎬ Cable laying visual - Mounted & foot drill &c.	
	8		⎭	
	9		31 Divisional Artillery moved to BEAUVAL on way to join 2nd Corps. Cable section sent with them.	
	10		⎫	
	11		⎬ Training company; &c visual - Cable laying - foot mounted drill etc.	
	12		⎭	

Army Form C. 2118

WAR DIARY
or
INTELLIGENCE SUMMARY

(Erase heading not required.)

Instructions regarding War Diaries and Intelligence Summaries are contained in F.S. Regs., Part II. and the Staff Manual respectively. Title Pages will be prepared in manuscript.

Place	Date	Hour	Summary of Events and Information	Remarks and references to Appendices
BERNAVILLE	7&6/13		Signal School moved to BERNAVILLE	
"	14		Bde Sections rejoined their Brigades. 2/Lt A.J. WATTS taking command of No 2 Section from Lt LION	
"	15.		normal work.	
"	16.			
"	17.			
"	18		92nd Bde moved to BEAUVAL on way to take over "Line" from 19th Div	
"	19		93rd Bde to BEAUVAL - 92nd Bde to 19th Div area. Traffic via XIII Corps.	
BEAUVAL	20		Div HQrs closed 12 noon & opened BEAUVAL same hour.	
AUTHIE	21	2 pm	" " AUTHIE " Traffic to Bde	
			Div 19 (W) Division has handed over command of the Sector 3. Div was to take over.	
"	22	6 am	3rd Div assumed command of line from 19th Division. Through hole at Saun & 92nd & 93rd Bdes in the line at Sailly & BAYENCOURT	

1875 Wt. W593/826 1,000,000 4/15 J.B.C. & A. A.D.S.S./Forms/C. 2118.

Army Form C. 2118

WAR DIARY
or
INTELLIGENCE SUMMARY
(Erase heading not required.)

Instructions regarding War Diaries and Intelligence Summaries are contained in F. S. Regs., Part II. and the Staff Manual respectively. Title Pages will be prepared in manuscript.

Place	Date	Hour	Summary of Events and Information	Remarks and references to Appendices
AUTHIE	23rd		Above traffic via 19th Div till 10am when transferred direct to AUTHIE. Came under command of V Corps to tactical purposes. Moving telegraph circuits formed. V Corps, XIII Corps, 92 Bde, 93 Bde, 94 Bde, 19th Div. Normal telephone lines.	
	24th		Arranging office and opening report centre at COIGNEAU. Normal work until 8pm when information being received enemy to be withdrawing caused abnormal traffic.	
	25th	3am	Two cable detachments left one for 92nd Bde other for 93rd Bde.	
		7am	Cable detachments withdrawn. Very heavy telegraph, telephone + DR traffic.	
	26th		Twelve Corps Cavalry D.R.s reported for duty. The roads being almost impassable for motor cyclists.	
	27th		Ordered to move to COUIN by 2pm 1st March. Record telegraph	

WAR DIARY
or
INTELLIGENCE SUMMARY

(Erase heading not required.)

Army Form C. 2118

Place	Date	Hour	Summary of Events and Information	Remarks and references to Appendices
AUTHIE	28		Traffic 1153 messages through Office. Roads almost impassable for motor cyclists - mounted DR's being employed. Two heavy winders on Wilson control set fixed division. The later being Stable, used at HEBUTERNE. Two power buzzers and amplifier in use from 5th Army wireless. Amplifier at Stations at HEBUTERNE.	
			Appendix 18 gives month traffic record.	App 18
			" 19 " straight line diagram Communication Order 255.	App 19

J.A.F.Mann Capt.
O.C. 31 Div. Signal Coy. R.E.

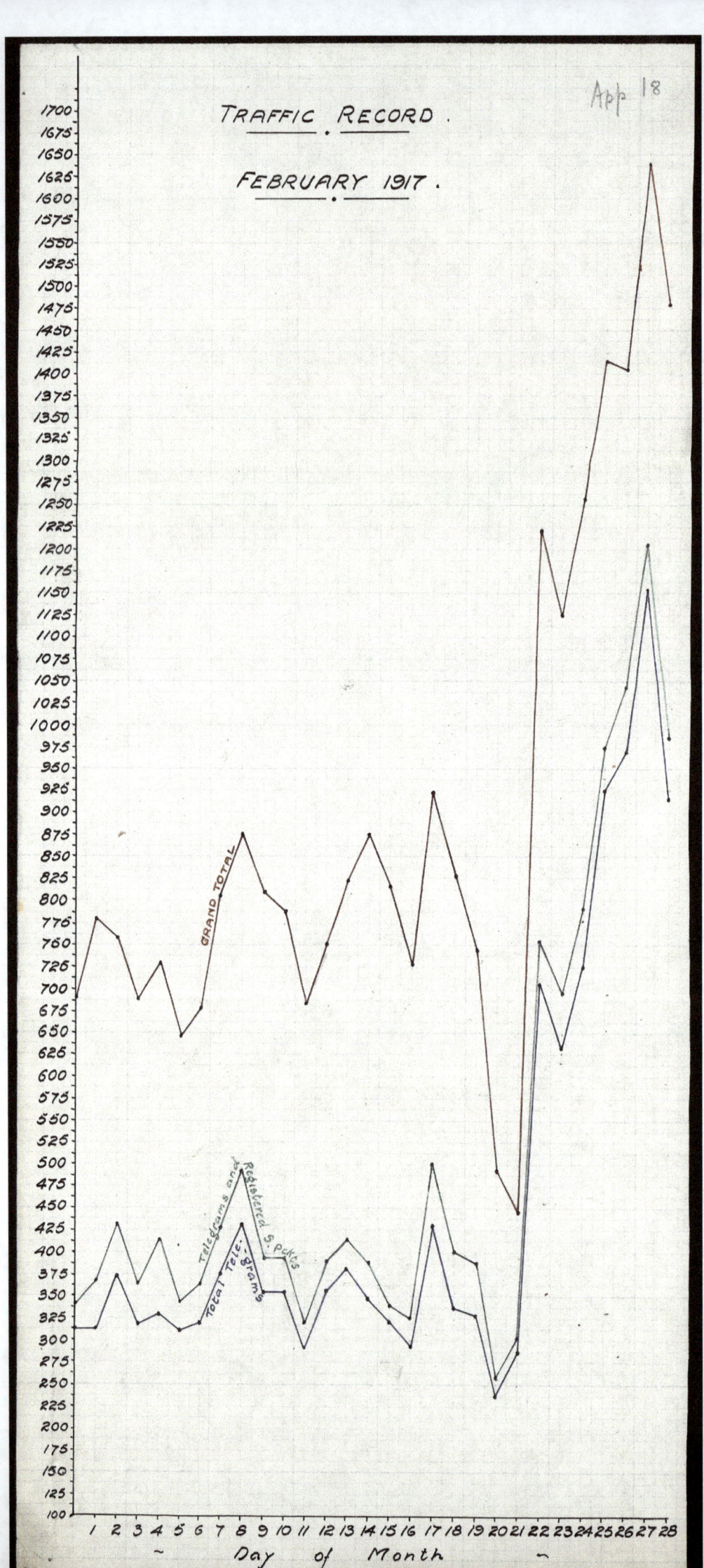

App 19

XA Communications Feb-March 1917

- Bde — Bayencourt
- Bde — Sailly
  - Phone (between the two Bdes)
- 165 Arty Bde — phone — Rep. Ctre
- 170 Arty Bde — phone — Rep. Ctre
- Bayencourt Bde — superimposed phone — Rep. Ctre (Coigneux)
- Sailly Bde — superimposed phone — Rep. Ctre
- CRE — Rep. Ctre
- St Léger Div Arty — phone / sounder — Rep. Ctre
- Rep. Ctre — sounder / phone — 31 Div H.Qrs AUTHIE
- 19th Divn (Couin) — superimposed — 31 Div AUTHIE
- 5th Corps (Acheux) — Sounder — 31 Div AUTHIE
- Bde (Thièvres) — superimposed — 31 Div AUTHIE
  - D.A.C.
- To XIII Corps Doullens — superimposed — 31 Div AUTHIE

LOCALS
- GOC
- G
- Q
- Dv Train
- Operating Stn.
- O.C. Sigs
- Phonograms
- FPO

Confidential

Volume XV

Vol /3

War Diary.

31st Divisional Signal Company. R.E.

March 1917.

Army Form C. 2118

WAR DIARY
or
INTELLIGENCE SUMMARY

(Erase heading not required.)

Instructions regarding War Diaries and Intelligence Summaries are contained in F. S. Regs., Part II. and the Staff Manual respectively. Title Pages will be prepared in manuscript.

31st SIGNAL COY R.E.

MARCH 1917   Summary of Events and Information

Place	Date	Hour	Summary of Events and Information	Remarks and references to Appendices
AUTHIE	1st		Roads East of COIGNEAU impassable for motor cyclists. DRs beyond this being carried on with mounted men.	
	2nd		94th Bde relieved 93rd Bde in the line	
	3rd		Moved advanced exchange from COIGNEAU to SAILLY.	
COUIN	4th		Div HQ moved to COUIN. Time of move 2pm. 92nd Bde took over from 19th Div front. With Bde HQ at WATERLOO BRIDGE.	
	5th		94th Bde moved from SAILLY to "APPLE TREES" taking over the 7th divisional front.	
	6th		Considerable trouble with the lines to 92nd and 94th Bdes owing to earthy lines in the armies. All D.R.s being carried out by mounted DRs	
	7th		Lt Bagley with party Advt moved to HEBUTERNE to build a 12 line route to Bde toward BUCQUOY.	
	8th		Building the route 75 pairs to on 94th front	
	9th		92nd Bde moved advanced HQ at ROSSIGNOL WOOD. Lais armoured [cable]...	

Army Form C. 2118

WAR DIARY
or
INTELLIGENCE SUMMARY
(Erase heading not required.)

Instructions regarding War Diaries and Intelligence Summaries are contained in F.S. Regs., Part II. and the Staff Manual respectively. Title Pages will be prepared in manuscript.

Place	Date	Hour	Summary of Events and Information	Remarks and references to Appendices
COVIN	10		Thin cable from HE 13 BUTTERNE to ROSSIGNOL WOOD working direct phone and superimposed sounder. 94th Bde moves to advanced HQ at PUSIEUX.	
"	11		Worked to 94th Bde via APPLE TREES Exchange.	
"	12		Rossignol Wood lines and Puisieux lines being broken by shell fire continually. Recovering all possible cable.	
"	13		Heavier arty fire front 46 Div and 7th Div, the artillery thinning in the line as before.	
"	14		Reeling in and clearing up all possible cable.	
"	15		— do —	
"	16		Warned to be ready to move at 4 hours notice to support attack on any portion of V Corps front.	
"	17		Standing by to do so on 18th.	
"	18		Packing preparatory to moving to 5th Army Area.	

Army Form C. 2118

WAR DIARY
or
INTELLIGENCE SUMMARY
(Erase heading not required.)

Instructions regarding War Diaries and Intelligence Summaries are contained in F.S. Regs., Part II. and the Staff Manual respectively. Title Pages will be prepared in manuscript.

Place	Date	Hour	Summary of Events and Information	Remarks and references to Appendices
Corin	19th		Division commenced to move by march to 1st Army Area	
BOUQUE-MAISON	20	10 a.m.	Closed H.Q. at Corin opened at BOUQUEMAISON at 12 noon. Telegraph and telephone to XIX Corps. Communication to Bdes. and RA by despatch rider.	
RAMECOURT	21st	10 a.m.	Closed HQ at BOUQUEMAISON and opened at RAMECOURT 12 noon. Communication as on 20th.	
PERNES	22nd	10 a.m.	Closed HQ at RAMECOURT and opened at PERNES at 12 noon. Communication as on 20th and 21st.	
"	23rd		Halted at PERNES	
NORRENT FONTES	24th	10 a.m.	Closed HQ at PERNES and opened at NORRENT FONTES at 12 noon. Telegraph and telephone to XIII Corps to Bdes and RA by DR	
ST VENANT	25th	10 a.m.	Closed HQ at NORRENT FONTES and opened 12 noon at ST VENANT, Telephone and Telegraph opens to XIII Corps, 92 Bde at ROBECQ.	

Army Form C. 2118

WAR DIARY
or
INTELLIGENCE SUMMARY
(Erase heading not required.)

Place	Date	Hour	Summary of Events and Information	Remarks and references to Appendices
ST VENANT			March 1917 Con'd	
			and 94 Bde at MERVILLE. 93rd Bde attached to 66 Division and 3. Divisional Artillery to 5th Canadian Corps. The detachment and two extra Linemen moved with Artillery H.Q. Billeting arrangements at ST VENANT most unsatisfactory, the huts and cookhouses being 20 minutes walk from the Signal Office.	
	26th			
"	27th		H.Q. of Signal Coy moved to huts closer to Signal Office. The division in G.H.Q. Reserve ready to move 91 at 24 hours notice.	
"	28th		Cleaning wagons checking Equipment etc.	
	29th		Normal work.	
	30			
	31			

Appendix 20 gives traffic records for the month. App. 20

[signature] OC 3rd Signal Coy R.E.

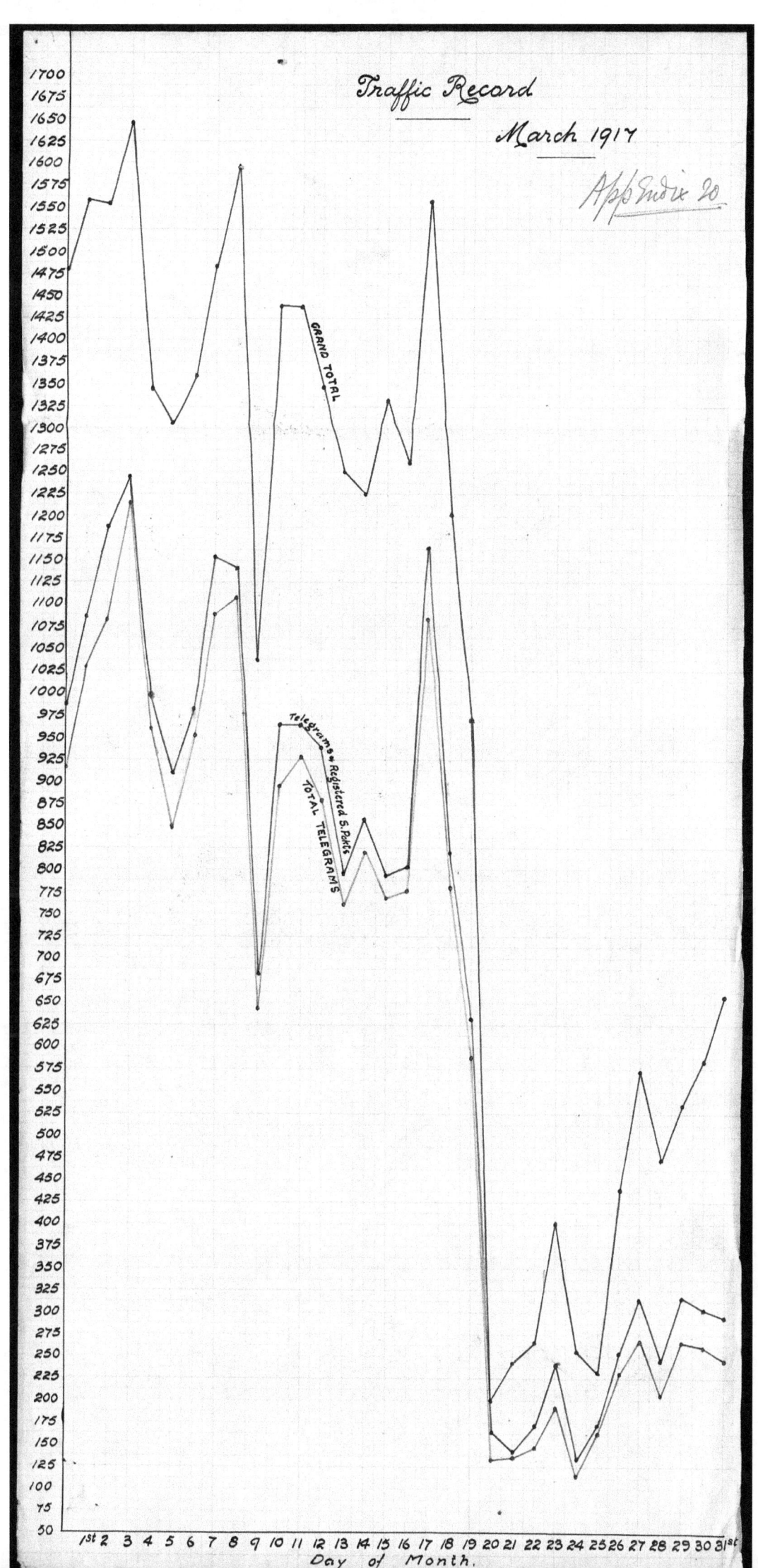

Confidential

Volume XVI
Vol 14

War Diary.

31st. Division Signal Coy. R.E.

April 1917.

WAR DIARY or INTELLIGENCE SUMMARY

Army Form C. 2118

31st DIV SIGNAL COY. R.E.

Place	Date	Hour	Summary of Events and Information	Remarks and references to Appendices
ST VENANT	April 1st		Normal Routine work.	
"	2nd to 7th		"	
"	8th		Liason with 17 OR. Proceeded to MARLES LES MINES to open advanced office. 92nd Bde moved to ALLOUAGNE, 94th Bde to GONNEHEM. Packed and ready to move at 4 hours notice.	
"	9th		Signal Coy moved to Auchel; details remain at St Venant for duty at St Venant office	
"	10th		MARLES LE MINES advanced office closed down at 1.0 p.m. D.H.Q. closed at ST VENANT at 2 p.m. & opened at BRUAY at 3/0 p.m. Signal Coy moved to BRUAY & took over communications from 63rd Div	
BRUAY	11th		92nd Bde at BRUAY, 93rd Bde at BETHUNE, 94th Bde at HOUCHIN. Communication established to 92nd Bde, 93rd Bde at BETHUNE, 94th Bde direct, to 94th Bde thro the Bruay Civil exchange.	
"	12th		Normal routine work. 93rd moved from Bethune to BARLIN; Communication by telephone & telegraph established	

WAR DIARY or INTELLIGENCE SUMMARY

Army Form C. 2118

31st Divl Signal Coy. R.E.

Place	Date	Hour	Summary of Events and Information	Remarks and references to Appendices
BRUAY	APRIL 1917 13th		92nd Bde. moved from BRUAY to DIEVAL. 93rd Bde. moved from BARLIN to FREVILLERS. 94th Bde. moved from HOUCHIN to BAJUS. Advanced signal office opened at Chateau Jenby near Ourton where communication was obtained to 93rd, 94th Bde; 92nd Bde by party.	
"	14th		4th Anti Bruay office to advanced office. Control work.	
OURTON	15th		D.H.Q. closed at Bruay at 12 noon; opened at Chateau Jenby near Ourton at same time. Main signal office opened near D.H.Q. with out office in OURTON for local circuits, telephonic & telegraphic communication opened direct to all brigades and advanced First Army, N.Corps working intermediate on advanced army circuit. Cable. Finished D5" laid out by cable wagons from D.H.Q signal office to 94th Bde. and OURTON office.	
"	16th		Normal routine work.	

Army Form C. 2118

WAR DIARY
or
INTELLIGENCE SUMMARY

(Erase heading not required.)

Instructions regarding War Diaries and Intelligence Summaries are contained in F. S. Regs., Part II. and the Staff Manual respectively. Title Pages will be prepared in manuscript.

Summary of Events and Information 31st Div. Signal Coy R.E.

Place	Date	Hour	Summary of Events and Information	Remarks and references to Appendices
OURTON	April 1917			
	17th		Normal routine work	
"	18th		Normal routine work	
"	19th		Visual by Helio & Lucas lamps established to Inf. Bde. H.Q. & the three brigades	
"	20th		Normal routine work	
"	21st		Normal routine work; practice cable laying carried out by cable Sections	
"	22nd		Normal routine work	
"	23rd		Normal routine work.	
"	24th		92nd Bde. move from DIEVAL to VILLERS CHATEL	
"	25th 26th 27th		Normal routine work	
"	28th		92nd Bde. move from VILLERS CHATEL to MAROEUIL. Cable sections made to 63rd Div. area for erection of new routes 93rd Bde. move from FREVILLERS to ECOIVRES. X HUTS.	
VILLERS CHATEL	29		D.H.Q. move from O.1.O.B. to VILLERS CHATEL 94th Bde. move from BAJUS to FREVILLERS	

Army Form C. 2118

WAR DIARY
or
INTELLIGENCE SUMMARY
(Erase heading not required.)

3rd Div. Signal Coy. R.E.

Place	Date	Hour	Summary of Events and Information	Remarks and references to Appendices
About 2½ miles NE of Arras.	30th		93rd Inf. Bde takes over Line from 188th Inf. Bde - come under orders of 63rd Division. D.H.Q move from VILLERS CHATEL to H.Q. of 63rd Division at G4 A0H & open at 10 A.M. taking over Line from 63rd Division. Communication established to Inf. Bdes. Many new routes built from future H.Q. to old buried system. Appendix 21 gives traffic diagram for month.	App 21

J. A. Allen Capt.
No. 3. Divisional Signal Co.
O.C. 3. Divisional R.E.

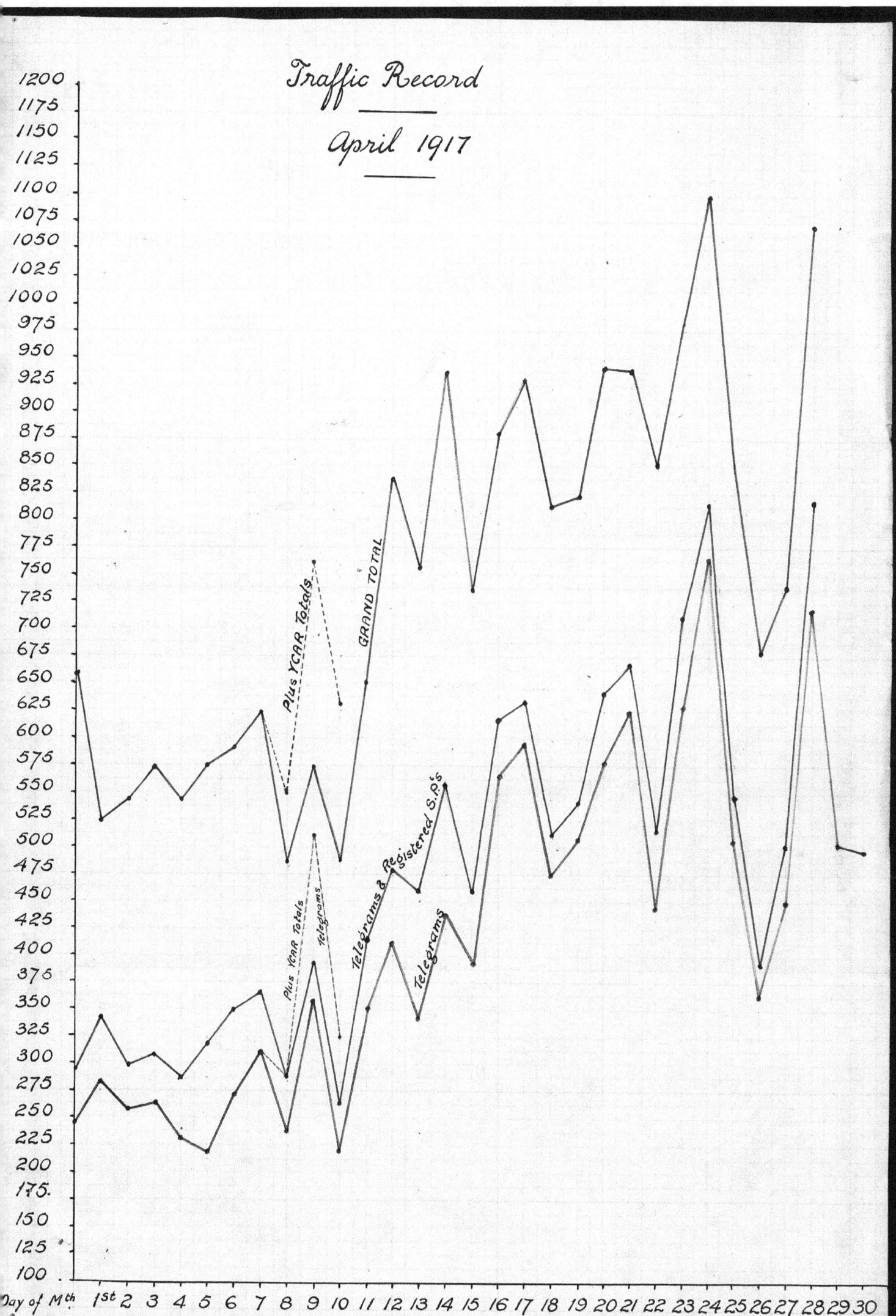

Confidential

Volume XVII

Vol 15

War Diary.

31st Divisional Signal Company. R.E.

May 1917.

Army Form C. 2118

WAR DIARY
or
INTELLIGENCE SUMMARY

(Erase heading not required.)

31st Dw. Signal Coy. R.E.

Place	Date	Hour	Summary of Events and Information	Remarks and references to Appendices
Nº Roellncourt	May 1917			
	1st		Land armoured cable from Bois de la Maison Blanche to 92nd Bde HQ just west of Bailleul	
	2nd		At 12 noon C.R.A. 31st Div took over Artillery Control on the divisional front with 9 artillery brigades. At 12 noon C.R.A. 31st Div moved to G.5.B.28 and opened at 5 p.m. 94th Inf Bde moved from G.4.A.16 to G.5.O.26 and opened at 10 p.m. Visual station very successful established near D.H.Q for emergency communication direct to advanced 93rd B.H.Q. Armoured cable laid from Bois de la Maison Blanche to advanced 93rd B.H.Q at Hespateker. During 1st & 2nd all forward communications for 93rd Bde renewed with armoured cable as forward communications had been cut in a very bad condition.	
	3rd	3-4-5 A.M.	Division attacked at 3-4-5 A.M. For details of communications, instructions, and report of working of communications during the attack see Appendix No. 22	
	4th		94th Bde relieved 92nd Bde in left sector. 92nd Bde to Gut camp	
	5th to 7th		Forward & backward wires cut by enemy shelling of gun positions. Normal work	

WAR DIARY or INTELLIGENCE SUMMARY

Army Form C. 2118

31st Div Signal Coy R.E.

Place	Date	Hour	Summary of Events and Information	Remarks and references to Appendices
Nº Roclincourt	MAY 1917			
	8th		Portion of our front in left sector handed over to 2nd Div. 94th Bde relieved 9 2nd Bde in Left sector. Twelve tons trunk route completed from D.H.Q. to B.19.D.38 + from point into war to Left Bde H.Q. Signal Office opened at St Catherine's; ten lines bull exchange rotunda installed.	
	9th		Armoured turns laid in old German lines	
	10th		Normal routine work	
	11th		Contour survey shelling of area between right battalion of Left Bde + Bde H.Q. destroys all ground lines; power buzzers used successfully	
	12th		Normal routine work	
	13th		92nd Bde relieve 93rd Bde in right sector at 10p.m.	
	14th		Testing of old German buried cable in right sector carried out without success	
	15th		Normal routine work	
	16th		Lateral cable laid from Right Brigade to Left Bde. of Division on right	

Army Form C. 2118

WAR DIARY
or
INTELLIGENCE SUMMARY
(Erase heading not required.)

Instructions regarding War Diaries and Intelligence Summaries are contained in F. S. Regs., Part II. and the Staff Manual respectively. Title Pages will be prepared in manuscript.

31st Div. Signal Coy R.E.

Place	Date	Hour	Summary of Events and Information	Remarks and references to Appendices
	MAY 1917			
Near Bavincourt	17th		93rd Inf. Bde. relieved 92nd Inf. Bde. in right sector on night of 16/17th. Normal work	
	18th		Normal work	
	19th		Preparations made for relief of Division by 63rd (R.N.) Division. Revised instructions issued in connection with warning of gas attacks.	
	20th		On night of 19th/20th 93rd Inf. Bde. relieved by 188th Inf. Bde. of 63rd Div.	
	21st		Handed over to 63rd Div. at 10 A.M. opened at VILLERS CHATEL at main Row. See attached diagrams instructions in connection with communications handed over to incoming division. On night of 20th/21st 94th Inf. Bde. relieved by 190th Inf. Bde. in left sector. Communication established at new office by telegraph to XIII Corps + 94th Inf. Bde. at MONT ST ELOY.	
VILLERS CHATEL	22nd 26th			
	27th		94th Bde. exchanged accommodation with 93rd Bde.	
	28-31st		Normal routine work	

J Hutchinson Capt
for O.C. 31st Div. Signal Coy
R.E.

SECRET.   Appendix No 22   COPY NO......

SIGNAL INSTRUCTIONS IN CONJUNCTION WITH
31st DIVISION ORDER NO.139.

2.5.17

1. Throughout the Operations all wires will be reserved exclusively for tactical messages, all others being disposed of as opportunity occurs. All but tactical Subscribers to the telephone exchanges, (see list attached) are requested to make their conversation as brief as possible, in order to save congestion and delay.

2. Where both telegraph and telephone circuits exist to a unit in the event of the one breaking down, the remaining one will be used for telegraph.

3. G.Os.C.Brigades will attach additional personnel to assist Brigade Section Signal Officers, according to their requirements.

4. Telephone.
   The attached list gives the Subscribers on each Exchange and all Exchanges are connected together.
   Telegraph.
   To 92nd Brigade, 93rd Brigade, Corps, 94th Brigade, ST.CATHERINE'S. To battalions in action from Brigades.

5. Lines.
   There are no buried cables forward of Divisional Headquarters. All wires are "airline" as far as the line through B.25 Central, H.I Central. East of this they are surface cables and where possible are laid in trenches.

6. Runners and Orderlies.
   All runners will carry their messages in their right hand breast pocket and all ranks must be instructed to search all runner casualties for any messages that may be on them.
   The O.C. Brigade Signal Sections will arrange a Brigade chain of relay posts to Brigade Forward Signal Stations.
   The relay system is employed from Divisional Headquarters to Brigades with the following relay posts :-
   To the 93rd Brigade; relay posts at Bois de la Maison Blanche and H.3.d.5.6. (By motor cyclists and mounted D.R. to the former and by runner thence to the latter).
   All 92nd Brigade messages are sent through a joint 31st and 2nd Divisional relay system with relay posts at A.30.a.48., B.19.d.28., B.20.b.14 to Brigade.

7. Wireless.   93rd Sector.
   One trench set at Advanced Brigade Headquarters (H.3.d.5.6.) and another trench set at Bois de la Maison Blanche. Both, in addition to communicating with their control set at ROCLINCOURT, which is in direct telephonic communication with Divisional Headquarters, can also work to each other.

   92nd Brigade Sector.
   One Trench set at Brigade Headquarters working to control set at ROCLINCOURT.

Brigades will

- 2 -

Brigades will detail one Officer and 6 men to be with the Wireless set. The Officer will encode and decode messages and the 6 men will move the apparatus forward if required to do so.

8. <u>Power Buzzers.</u>   <u>93rd Brigade Sector.</u>

There is a Power Buzzer and Amplifier at Advanced Brigade Headquarters, H.3.d.5.6. working to a Power Buzzer and Amplifier at Brigade forward station B.29.c.2.2. These work to a Power Buzzer and Amplifier at Battalion Headquarters B.24.c.8.0. There is also a Power Buzzer at Battalion Headquarters B.30.c.4.8. working to either the Amplifier at Brigade forward Station or to Battalion at B.24.c.8.0.

<u>92nd Brigade Sector.</u>

One Power Buzzer and one Amplifier at B.17.d.2.4. receiving from two Power Buzzers (of which one will go forward with each Battalion) and working back to an Amplifier and Power Buzzer at Brigade Headquarters at B.21.a.8.8.

9. <u>Pigeons.</u>

20 pigeons are available for each Brigade. Of these 6 birds will go forward with attacking Companies of each Battalion; 4 will be at attacking Battalion Headquarters and the remainder held in reserve, the position to be selected by Brigade Signal Officers.

10. <u>Visual.</u>

All Signallers with attacking troops, when signalling back will send their messages "D.D" and slowly. They must face the high ground directly behind them.

If this is done the signals will be read by either Brigade Visual Stations at H.3.d.36., B.21.a.8.8. or by Divisional stations at B.20.b.1.8. Each of these stations is in direct telephone and telegraph communication with Division.

11. <u>Stores.</u>

The supply of cable is very limited and all units must ensure economy. Main cable and signal store dumps will be formed at each Brigade Headquarters and at Bois de la Maison Blanche.

12. <u>Message Cards.</u>

Will be used whenever possible.

Lieut.-Colonel.
General Staff.

2.5.17.

Copy to all recipients of Division Order 139.

DIVISION EXCHANGE.

XIII Corps Exchange.
31st Div. Artillery Exchange.
92nd Brigade Exchange.
93rd Brigade Advanced Exchange.
94th Brigade Exchange.
"G" Branch.
"Q" Branch.
C. R. E.
O.C. Signals.
Signal Master.
2nd Division Exchange.
9th Division Exchange.
XIII Corps O.P.
31st Div. O.P.
93rd Brigade Rear Exchange.

94th BRIGADE EXCHANGE.

Brigade Major.
Wireless Directing Station.
A. D. M. S.
210th Field Company.
Divisional Train.
63rd D. A. C.
L.R.X. Exchange.
31st Division.

MAISON BLANCHE EXCHANGE.

Staff Captain.
93rd Bde. Advanced Exchange.
Rib.
Check.
Canvas.
Deck.
Test Pair.
31st Division.

DIRECT PHONES.

31st Division "G" - XIII Corps "G"
31st Divisional R.A. - XIII Corps R.A.

DIVISIONAL ARTILLERY EXCHANGE

XIII Corps R.A.
Brigade Major.
Staff Captain.
2nd Div. R.A. Exchange.
223rd Bde. R.F.A.
311th Bde. R.F.A.
86th Bde. R.F.A.
317th Bde. R.F.A.
64th Bde. R.F.A.
165th Bde. R.F.A.
34th Bde. R.F.A.
A. R. P.
80th H.A.G.
Wagon Lines.

REPORT ON COMMUNICATIONS DURING OPERATIONS MAY 3rd.

DIVISIONAL.

General.

All preparations were rushed, only 66 hours were available for work prior to the attack, which included taking over a Divisional Front, side-slipping at short notice on a Brigade Front to the North and a move of Divisional Headquarters.

Infantry Communications taken over were unreliable, having been badly cut about. There was insufficient time to bury cables satisfactorily or to learn the safest routes over which to lay ground wires; However, alternate routes were laid to each Infantry Brigade as far as possible along old German trenches and 93rd Brigade forward Sector was rewired. Neither telephone nor telegraph completely broke down to Brigades, which was largely due to the excellent work of the linesmen who were posted at intervals along the routes, repairing a broken one, whilst work was carried on on another.

Visual.

Divisional Stations, which were kept manned day and night, were not made use of or required.

Wireless.

This was several times used between Brigades and Division during the 2nd and 4th May, when wires were cut.

Runners.

The Runner Relay system to the left Brigade Headquarters was worked in conjunction with the 2nd Division. It was considered more advisable, owing to the short time available, to work posts through this system, which was known to be in working order, rather than to commence a new system with new men.

The post to this Brigade was very slow and since a new one has been started the time taken for the outward and return post has been reduced by 9 hours.

(461 D.R. packets passed through the office during the day.)

Telephone.

Telephone traffic throughout the 3rd was very much lower than anticipated, but telegraph was normal, 725 wires passing through the Divisional Office.

92nd BRIGADE SECTOR.

The existing wires in the Sector, as taken over, were used and were kept through, except for short intervals, to Battalions. Forward of battalions it was impossible to maintain wires.

Power Buzzer.

The power buzzers sent forward with the right battalion would not work during the attack. This was probably due to want of training and experience in the technical working and laying of earth wires. The stationery power buzzer and amplifier proved satisfactory, but no actual messages were sent by them, it not being necessary as telephone wires were usually through.

Runners.

22 were employed at Brigade Headquarters and considered by 92nd Brigade to be insufficient. 30 were employed with each battalion.

Pigeons.

One message was sent from a Company Headquarters and reached the Brigade in 30 minutes.

Visual.

Although Brigade stations were manned day and night no messages were received from forward troops, but this is probably owing to the morning mist, smoke and dust, Oppy Wood being frequently hidden from view.

93rd BRIGADE SECTOR.

Forward wires were relaid and all the cables held up, until about an hour after Zero, after which time they were being continually cut, but no battalion was out of telephonic communication for more than half an hour, lines being relaid by linesmen at relay posts.

Power Buzzers.

There were four power buzzers and three amplifiers in the Sector. Of the two forward power buzzers, the one was not required for use, as the cable to the battalion remained intact the whole time, and the other worked very well and sent seven messages, of which four were S.O.S. calls and three were calls to lengthen barrage.

Runners.

44 were employed at Brigade Headquarters and Brigade Runner posts and it was found that this number was just sufficient. One battalion employed 74 runners which were not considered excessive, whereas battalions of the 92nd Brigade only employed 30 each.

Pigeon Messages.

2 were sent (of which one was a map) from Battalion Headquarters and took 2 hours to reach Brigade.

Visual.

Was not used at all.

ARTILLERY COMMUNICATIONS.

9 Artillery Brigades were covering the Divisional Front under C.R.A. 31st Division.

Beyond improving laterals it was impossible to make any improvement to the existing communications, all available time being spent in learning the existing system. As far as I am able to ascertain the communications throughout the R.A. were quite satisfactory.

SUMMARY AND SUGGESTIONS.

Lateral communications appear to have required improvement.

Power Buzzers.

These undoubtedly proved themselves satisfactory and on future occasions should, I think, be used more for the Artillery and Infantry Liaison work, as messages sent seem to have been confined mainly to S.O.S. and barrage calls.

Pigeons.

For the first time in this Division pigeons were used with success, but a large number of birds were released without messages and the messages sent by this service were more from Battalion Headquarters than from Companies. On one occasion a map was sent back by 18th W.Yorks, and it would possibly appear to be a good idea for Company Commanders to have drawn, beforehand, on a pigeon message form, a rough map of the locality to which he is going. He could then mark in his position, time it, and this would save writing things out on thin rice paper, which is bound to be difficult under the conditions.

Runners.

Owing to the type of ground to work over it is essential to have 12 to 16 runners employed on a runner post between Division and Brigades.

There appears to be considerable difference in the numbers employed by various units. This, I think, is mainly due to want of arranging a sound relay system in each sector and all runners from forward units being fully conversant with the various posts; Battalions frequently running direct back to Brigade instead of to forward posts of the relay system.

Visual.

This requires encouragement and more personnel than can at present be spared. Artillery are using visual considerably more than the Infantry and with success.

Liaison.

The increase in the number of guns and the growing number of Liaison Officers points to the desirability of a separate and independent liaison communication system on a bigger scale than at present.

(sgd) F. Mair

Major
O.C. 31st Divisional Signal Coy R.E.

10.5.1917

SECRET

FORWARD COMMUNICATIONS.
3ST DIVISION
— KEY DIAGRAM —

SHEET 51B N.W.   1:20000

Key:
- ▬▬▬ Airline
- ▬▬▬ Ground cable
- ········ Visual
- ∿∿∿ Wireless
- ∿⎯∿ Power Buzzer & Amplifier.

- ♛ Divisional H.Qrs.
- ▲ Brigade H.Qrs.
- ▲ Advcd. Bde. H.Qrs.
- ⌐ Linesman's Post (Test Dug-out)
- ◯ Wireless Station
- W Wireless Station
- ✦ Power Buzzer
- A Amplifier Station
- ⊕ Visual Station
- R Runner station / Runner relay post
- Y Pigeon Station or loft.

SECRET.

DETAILS OF DEFENSE SIGNAL
COMMUNICATIONS 31ST DIVISION.
(Corrected to 18. 5. 1917.)

CONTENTS.

Page 1.	Position 1
" 2.	Position 1.
" 3.	Position 2 & 3.
" 4.	Position 4, 5, 6, 7,
" 5.	Position 8, 9, 10, 11.
" 6.	Position 12, 13, 14.
" 7.	Position 15, 16, 17, 18, 19, 20, 21, 22, 23,
" 8.	Position 24, 25, 26.
" 9.	Position 27, 28.
" 10.	Rear Communications.
Appendix I.	Circuit List.
" II.	Telegraph Circulation List.
" III.	Key Diagram.

:-:-:-:-:-:-:-:-:-:-

DETAILS OF COMMUNICATION ARRANGEMENTS IN 31ST DIVISION AREA.

N.B. Numbers inside circle thus ⑤ are reference to Key Diagram attached.

DIVISIONAL HEADQUARTERS.

①

TELEGRAPH.
    Sounder to 2 Brigades in the line.
    Sounder to 1 Brigade in rest.
    2 Sounders to XIII Corps.
    1 Sounder to Right Division.
    1 Sounder to St Catherine.
    1 Buzzer to Left Brigade.

TELEPHONE. 30 Line Exchange.

1. 6th Brigade.
2. Divl Train(2 rings.) D.A.D.O.S.(3 rings.)
3. Maison Blanche Exchange.
4. 17th Division(Advced.)
5. 188th Brigade.
6. Buzzer Junction R.A.
7. 94th Inf.Brigade.
8. Left Division(5th)
9. L.R.X. Exchange.
10. F.C. Exchange.
11. 189 Brigade.
12.
13.
14. Maison Blanche Exchange.
15. St Catherine Exchange.
16.
17. G.Branch.
18. Corps.
19. G Branch.
20. Q Branch.
21. O.C. Signals.
22. C.R.E.
23. G.O.C.
24. Signal Master.
25. Divl Artillery.
26.
27. Corps.
28. C.R.E. 63rd Division
29.
30. 94th Inf Brigade.

SEALED PACKETS.
    D.R.L.S. posts 3 times daily to all units at 8 a.m. 2 p.m. 8 p.m.

(a) To Right Brigade ② by mounted D.R.
(b) To Left Brigade ⑤ by mounted D.R. to Right Brigade, thence by runner to relay post ⑧ thence left Brigade at ③
(c) To Corps. At 7 a.m. 12 noon, 7 p.m. by Motor Cyclist.
(d) To back area. At 8 a.m. 2 p.m. 8 p.m. (St Catherine, Maroeuil etc.)
(e) Left Group R.A. To Right Brigade, thence to left Brigade from which the group collects.
(f) Right Group R.A. ② By mounted D.R.

WIRELESS.
    Messages phoned via 5th Division to control station ⑮ which transmits them to right or left Brigade Headquarter trench sets.

    The continuous wave set works direct to R.A. O.P. Exchange at ⑦

PIGEON.
    Pigeon messages received from MAROEUIL loft by wire from XIII Corps.

VISUAL. ㉖ Station only manned if all wires and wireless break down. Messages phoned to Visual Station.

ARTILLERY.

Joint office with main Divisional Office, but with separate bell and buzzer Exchanges.

BELL EXCHANGE.	BUZZER EXCHANGE.
1. Brigade Major R.A.	1. Capt Tayler.
2. Buzzer Junction.	2. 223rd & 317th Brigades.
3. XIII Corps.	3. " " Wagon Lines.
4. 223rd Brigade.	4. A.R.P.
5. Staff Captain.	5.
6. 317th Brigade.	6. 34th Brigade.
7. 31st Exchange Junction.	7. 165th Brigade Wag.Lines.
8. G.O.C. R.A.	8. 17th Divl Artillery.
9. 2nd Divl Artillery.	9. Telegrams.
10. 34th Brigade.	10. Telegrams.
	11. 31st Junction.
	12. 165th Brigade.
	13. 80th H.A.G.
	14. 170th Brigade.
	15. Mess.

PERSONNEL.

The whole Company and stores, except linesmen posted at out stations accommodated in vicinity of Headquarters.

WIRES.

Divisional Headquarters is known as C.A. for purposes of labelling.

Three airline routes leave CA

```
CA - FF   6 pairs
CA - TR  10 pairs.
CA - KS  12 pairs.
```

For details of connections see circuit list attached.

No. 2.

Right Brigade Rear Headquarters.

TELEPHONE.

    10 line Magneto Exchange.

1. 31st Division.   6. Buzzer Board.
2. 31st Division.   7. Linesman Test.
3. Brigade Major.   8.
4. Staff.   9.
5. Buzzer Board.   10.

TELEGRAPH.

Sounder to Division.
2 4 x 3 buzzer units.

1. Left Brigade.   1. Bell Exchange.
2. Adv. Headquarters.   2. Bell Exchange.
3. Battalion.   3. Staff Office.
4. Battalion.   4.
5. Battalion.   5.
6. M.G. Company.   6.
7. R.A. Group.   7.

WIRES.

Labelling position known as MB.
Airline to Division. To Flank Brigades and forward ground cables.

RUNNERS.

6 for work ato Left Brigade at position ③
4 for Brigade running to position ④

PERSONNEL.

Divisional linesmen. 1 N.C.O. 4 men.

Left Brigade Headquarters. "TY"

No. 3.

TELEPHONE.

    5 line Magneto Exchange.

1. Division.
2. Division.
3. Brigade Major.
4. Staff Captain.
5.

TELEGRAPH.

Sounder to Division.
3 4 x 3 buzzer units.

1. Division.   1. 170th Brigade R.F.S.
2. Right Brigade.   2. F.C.F. Brigade.
3. Left Brigade.   3. Junction to Magneto.
4. Left Brigade.   4.   "   " Liaison.
5. D. House.   5. Signals.
6. Left Brigade   6. Left Brigade R.C.
7. Left Brigade.   7.

WIRES.

All ground cables. Two alternate routes
(2 pairs on each) to Division.

RUNNERS.

Divisional Runners to Position ②
Brigade runners to position 20.

PERSONNEL.   2 Divisional linesmen.

POWER BUZZER.
AMPLIFIER.   Working to ⑭

WIRELESS.
                  Trench set working to Control Set ⑮.

Advanced Right Brigade HQ.

No 4.

1 buzzer 4 x 3 units.

1. Rear H.Q.
2. Battalion.
3. Right Brigade.
4. R.A. Exchange.
5. Staff Office.
6. M.G. Co (advanced)
7.

WIRES.   position for labelling known as H3, all ground cables.

RUNNERS.   2 Brigade men running to ⑩ and ②

PERSONNEL.   1 N.C.O. and 3 Brigade linesmen.

POWER BUZZER.
AMPLIFIER.   working to ⑩.

223rd R.F.A. Brigade O.P.

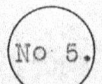

Visual Station working Battalion HQ ⑫ and ⑬ staffed by 3 signallers found by reserve battalion of brigade in the Sector.

165th R.F.A. Brigade O.P.

Visual station working to Battalion HQ at ⑬ and ⑫ staffed by 3 Corps Cavalry signallers and rationed by 165th Brigade.

Artillery Brigade O.P. Exchange.

1 Buzzer Unit.

1. 170th Brigade O.P.
2. 165th   "   "
3. 223rd   "   "
4. 317th   "   "
5. 83rd H.A.G. O.P. & Forward Exchange.
6. 233rd Brigade O.P.
7. 80th H.A.G. O.P. Exchange.

also 88th Heavy Brigade O.P. Exchange.

PERSONNEL.   1 Corporal and 4 gunners, of which 2 are operators from Heavy R.A. and 2 are gunner linesmen.

WIRELESS.
Continuous wave set working to Divisional Headquarters (1)
This set is more or less experimental and it is hoped to obtain wireless telephony between the two stations.

Linesmens' Test Point.

(No 8.)

2 Divisional linesmen. Test phone wire to (2) (These two men are rationed and accommodated by Field Coy R.E.)
6 Divisional runners.

(No 9.)

Left Group HQ and 170th R.F.A. Brigade O.P.

Visual station working to left battalion at (14). Personnel of 3 is found by Corps Cavalry signallers.
They are rationed by the R.F.A. Brigades.

TELEPHONE.

1 5 line Magneto Exchange.

1. Divl Artillery HQ.
2. 165th Brigade.
3.
4. Mess.
5. 34th Brigade.

2 4 x 3 Buzzer units.

1. A/Bty 170th Bde.   1. C/Bty 170th Bde.
2. B & D/Btys 170th Bde.   2. Adjutant.
3. C.O's Office.   3. Brigade O.P.
4. Brigade Office.   4.
5.   5.
6. 315th Brigade.   6. 94th Inf Brigade.
7.   D/170th Forward.
                             7. O.P. Exchange.

(No 10.)

Runner & linesman relay post belonging to Right Brigade.

4 runners work to Battalions at (11) and (12), also to Advanced Brigade HQ (4)

PERSONNEL.
1 N.C.O. and 3 Brigade linesmen.

POWER BUZZER. Double working to and receiving from
AMPLIFIER.   Power Buzzer advanced Brigade HQ (4)
               Battalion HQ (11).

Battalion HQ of Left Brigade.

(No 11)

Telephone & Telegraph.

Buzzer unit.

1. Brigade.
2. Support Battn.
3. Right Coy. of Support Battn.
4. Coy in line.
5.   "   "
6.
7.

POWER BUZZER.   Works to Amplifier at (10)

VISUAL.   Receives from Company HQ.

PIGEON.   Station consists of 2 birds.

Runners.   Work to relay post (10).

(No 12)
Support Battalion HQ of Left Brigade.

1 Buzzer Unit

1. Brigade.
2. Battn in line.
3. Coy.
4. Coy.
5. Battn Staff.
6.
7.

VISUAL.   Sends messages to visual station (5) manned by Battalion Signallers.

PIGEON.   Station of 2 birds.

RUNNERS.   Work to relay post (10).

(No 13)
Right Battalion HQ of Left Brigade.

1 Buzzer 4 x 3 units.

1. Brigade HQ.
2. Adjutant.
3. Artillery Group.
4.
5.
6.
7.

N.B.   Have been unable to maintain communication satisfactorily by wire to this position owing to the very heavy shelling.

VISUAL.   Station can sent to either Visual station at (6) or (5).

RUNNERS.   Work to relay post at (11)

POWER BUZZER.   double working to (14) thence to
AMPLIFIER.   Brigade. Receives from Power Buzzer at Windmill.

PIGEON.   Station of 2 birds.
The birds are sent up through the runner relay system.

(No 14)
Left Battalion HQ of Left Brigade.

Buzzer 4 x 3 units.

1. Brigade.   4. Pos. 21
2. Brigade.   5. Supply Column.
3. Brigade.   6. Liaison.
                   7. Signals.

VISUAL.   Station sends messages to (9)

RUNNERS.   Work to relay post at (21)

POWER BUZZER. double working to (13) and (3)
AMPLIFIER.

PIGEON.   Station of 2 birds.

(No 15)
              Wireless Control Set.

           In direct telephonic communication to 5th Division (16) working to trench sets at (2) and (3).

              Left Flank Divisional HQ.

(No 16)
          Direct telephonic line to Divisional H.Q. (1)
Telegraph via Corps.

              Right Flank Division. Adv: H.Q:

(No 17)
          Direct telephone and telegraph to Divisional HQ (1).

              Right Flank Brigade. Adv: H.Q.

(No 18)
          Direct lines to Right Advanced Brigade HQ (4).

              Left Flank Brigade.

(No 19)
          Direct telephone and telegraph lines to left Brigade at (3).

              Brigade Runner &
Lineman Post.

(No 20)
          4 Brigade Linesmen.

              Runner Relay Post
and Lineman Post.

(No 21)
          8 Brigade Runners.
          4   "   Linemen.

              No 5 Test Box.

(No 22)
          For circuits see circuit list attached.

(No 23)
              223rd Brigade H.Q.

          1 5 line Magneto Exchange.

      1. 317 F.A. Brigade.
      2. H.Q. Divl Artillery.
      3. 105th Brigade F.A.
      4. 152 F.A. Brigade.
      5.

No 23 contd.

HQ 223rd F.A. Brigade.

2 4 x 3 Buzzer Units.

1. A/Bty 223rd Bde.	1. Bde & Battn Liaison 1.
2. B/Bty 223rd Bde	2. " " " 2.
3. C/ " " "	3. O.P. Exchange.
4. D/ " " "	83rd H.A.G.
5. A & D detached Sect.	4. Staff Office.
17th D.A. Exchange.	5. Wireless.
6. Divl Arty,	6. Group Commander.
317th Bde Buzzer line.	7. Adjutant.
7. 311th Bde.	Office.

Linesmen's Room.

No 24.

HQ 317th F.A. Brigade.

1 5 line Magneto.

1. Right Inf. Brigade.
2. Left Group of Right Division.
3.
4. Divl Artillery.
5. 223rd F.A. Brigade.

2 4 x 3 Buzzer units.

1. A/Bty 317th Bde.	1. Brigade Commander.
2. B/ " " "	2. Wagon Lines.
3. C/ " " "	3.
4. D/ " " "	4.
5.	5. Office.
6.	6.
7. Adjutant.	7.

No 25.

HQ 165th R.F.A. Brigade.

1 5 line Magneto.

1. 170th R.F.A. Brigade.
2. 223rd F.A. Brigade.
3. 311th F.A.   "
4. 31 Divl R.A.
5. Staff Office.

2 4 x 3 Buzzer Boards.

1. A/Bty 165th Bde.	1. Adjutant.
2. B/ " " "	2. Staff Office.
3. C/Bty " "	3. Wagon Lines.
4. D/ " " "	4.
5.	5.
6.	6.
7. O.P. Exchange.	7. C.O. Brigade.

No 26.

H5 Test Point.

Airline on CA-TR joins buried cables.
10 pairs of wires on the CA-TR route.
(For details see circuit list attached.)

VISUAL. Is possible to near No 5 position, but this is only manned in the event of emergency when all wires and wireless are out of action.

No 27.   V Test Point.

       End of buried routes and commencement of the VBR airline. 12 pairs.
       For details of connections see circuit list attached.

No 28.   BR Junction Pole & Test Point.

       For details of connections see circuit list attached.

REAR COMMUNICATIONS.

Signal Offices at St Catherine, and G.4.a. Camp.

Telegraph to each and 10 line bell Exchange at each place.
(for subscribers see list of subscribers on Divisional Telephone System.)

LINES.

For details of circuits see Circuit List attached.

PERSONNEL.

St Catherine Office.

1 Motor Cyclist D.R.
1 N.C.O. i/c Office.
2 Operators.
1 linesman.

Units in the vicinity send to collect their telegrams and Sealed Packets from the office at various times during the day, except Priority wires which are delivered direct.

Vide Traffic Circulation list attached for deliveries from this office.

G.4.a. Office.

PERSONNEL.

Provided by Reserve Brigade.

Y. C. A. CIRCUITS.

Corps Super.	CATR 1&2 - H6 - C38 - MC 17&18 - MT 7 - MQ 1.
Corps G.	" 3&4 - H8 - C37 - MC 15&16 - MT10 - MQ2.
St Catherine Sup	" 5&6 - H13 - L23 - C16 - Y10 - Z20.
F.C. Super.	" 7&8 - H48 - L12 - FC5 & 6
Corps phone.	" 9&10 - H40 - L13 - BC9 - B1.
Corps R.A. &)	
Corps -YCA sdr)	" 11&12 - H39 - L33.
superimposed.)	
LRX	" 13 & 14 - H36.(backward.)
Spare	" 15 & 16.
RFA Buzzer)	
Omnibus.)	" 17&18. H36(Forward)- H1 - VBR 19 &20-then cable.
317 R.F.A.	" 19&20. H37 " -H8 -VBR 21&22 -BRMB 15&16 then cable.
165 Wagon Lines)	
St Nicholas.)	CAKS 1&2 - H5/11 - H37 - L24 - CD 33.
Wagon Lines	" 3&4 - H6 - H41 - LH15(C1 and cable at LRX. (BC1 - A1C ditto.
Maison Blanche phone.	" 5&6 - KSBR 5&6 - BRMB 11&12.
17th Div Arty.	" 7&8 - KSBR 7&8 - BRMB 13&14 then cable.
Corps O.P.	" 9&10 - KSBR 9&10 - BRMC 13&14.
17th Div Super.	" 11&12 - KSBR 11&12 - then cable.
TY phone via)	
Maison Blanche.)	" 13&14 - KSBR 13&14 - BRMB 1&2. then cable.
Maison Blanche super.)	" 15&16 - KSBR 15&16 - BRMB 7&8.
223rd RFA.	" 17&18 - KSBR 3&4 - then cable.
165 RFA.	" 19&20 - to KS then cable.
Spare to KS	" 21 & 22.
A.R.P.	" 23 & 24 - H35.
T.Y. Super.	CAFF 1 & 2 - FFDH 1 & 2 - DHTY 5.
5th Div phone.	" 3 & 4 - G18 - CB 4.
TY Buzzer.	" 5 & 6 - FFDH 17 & 18 - DHTY3.
64 RFA.	" 7 & 8 - " 15 & 16 and cable.
34 RFA.	" 9 & 10 - " 19 & 20 & cable.
34 RFA.	" 11 & 12 - " 21 & 22 & cable.
D.A.D.O.S. and)	
Div Train)	D5 cable to tee outside 5th Div then CB8 to
Maroeuil.)	Friday box, then G36.

SUB OFFICES.

St Catherine Exchange.

YCA super	Z10 - Y10 - C16 & L23 - H13 - CATR 5 & 6.
FC phone.	Z5 - Y9 - GEE - FC11 & 12.
A.D.M.S.	Local (cable.)
A.P.M.	Local (cable.)
63rd D.A.C.	Local (cable.)
31st D.A.C.	Z9 - Y19 - DA3.

F.C. Exchange.

Pioneers.	FC 1 & 2 to LRX then cable.
210th F.Co RE	Local (cable.)
YCA super	FC 5 & 6 - L12 - H48 - CATR 7 & 8.
Wireless DS	FC 9 & 10.
St Catherine	FC 11 & 12 - C22 - Y9 - Z5.
LRX.	FC 15 & 16.

Map Reference 51B.   TELEGRAPH CIRCULATION.   SECRET.

UNIT.	LOCATION.	DELIVERED FROM.
S.S.O. & HQ. Divl Train	Maroeuil	N.C.O.
D.A.D.O.S.	"	N.C.O.
Divl Burial Officer	H.1.C.3.9.	Maison Blanche.
A.P.M.	St Catherine.	S.C.
H.Q. D.A.C.	Anzin St Aubin	S.C.
E.A.A. Section.	do	S.C.
210th Field Co R.E.	G.4.A.26.	F.C.
211th Field Co R.E.	G.10.D.22	Y.C.A.
223 Field Co R.E.	G.B.9.55	S.C.
12th K.O.Y.L.I.	G.9.B.37	F.C.
No 31 Supply Col.	Maroeuil	N.C.O.
A.D.M.S.	St Catherine	S.C.
93rd F.Amb.	do	S.C.
94th F.Amb.	Anzin St Aubin	S.C.
95th F.Amb.	St Catherine	S.C.
41st Mob Vet Section	Maroeuil	N.C.O.
31st Divl Salvage Officer	St Catherine	S.C.
No 1 Co Divl Train	Maroeuil	N.C.O.
No 2 Co Divl Train	do	N.C.O.
No 3 Co Divl Train	Ecoivres (F.13.C.91.)	N.C.O.
No 4 Co Divl Train	Maroeuil Cemetery	N.C.O.
Details QM & T.O. 10 E.Yorks	G. 4 Camp	F.C.
" " 11 E.Yorks	do	F.C.
" " 12 E.Yorks	do	F.C.
" " 13th E Yorks	do	F.C.
" " 92 M.G.Co	Anzin St Aubin	St Catherine.
" " 92 T.M.Bty	Ecurie.	F.C.
" " 15 W.Yorks	G.9.D	St Catherine
" " 16 W.Yorks	G.9.D	S.C.
" " 18 W.Yorks	G.9.D.	S.C.
" " 18 D.L.I.	G.9.D.	S.C.
" " 93 M.G.Co	St Catherine	S.C.
" " 93 T.M.Bty	do	S.C.
" " 11 E.Lancs	G.4 Camp	F.C.
" " 12 York & Lancs.	G.9.B	F.C.
" " 13 "	do	F.C.
" " 14 "	do	F.C.
" " 94 M.G.Co	G.7.B.5.7.	St Catherine
" " 94 T.M.Bty	G.9.B.	F.C.
A.D.V.S.	Maroeuil	N.C.O.
Senior Chaplain	St Catherine	S.C.
Divl Water Officer	G.9.D.16	S.C.
R.E.Dump	Maroeuil	N.C.O.
341 Road Construction Co.	Ecurie	F.C.
483 Field Co	Ecurie	F.C.
349 Field Co		F.C.
176 Tunnelling Co	G.10.B.5.8.	F.C.
Advanced Divl Dump	B26 C.22	Maison Blanche
Main Divl Dump	G.9.C.7.8.	F.C.
C.Co Labour Battalion		St Catherine.
18th Cheshires.	Roclincourt	Y.C.A.
L.Co 1st Field Survey Co	G.9.B.3.7.	F.C.
247 Field Co R.E.	G.10.A.3.7.	F.C.
261 Railway Company R.E.		Y.C.A.
22nd Royal Fusiliers		Y.C.A.
23rd do do		Y.C.A.
1st Royal Berks		Y.C.A.
1st K.R.R.		

UNIT	LOCATION	DELIVERED FROM
63rd D.A.C.	Anzin St Aubin	S.C.
86th B.A.C.	do	S.C.
No 14 M.A.C.		S.C.
T Wireless Section		S.C.
Main Bomb Store	Billett 41 St Catherine	S.C.
French Mission	Maroeuil	N.C.O.
Howe Battalion		Y.C.A.
Anson Battalion		Y.C.A.
Hood Battalion		Y.C.A.
19th Labour Co, Queens		Y.C.A.
4th Labour Co, Devons.		Y.C.A.
16th Labour Co, Lincolns		Y.C.A.
56 Labour Co.	G.8.D.52	S.C.
11th Labour Co, Northants.		Y.C.A.
Divisional Gas Officer		Y.C.A.
C.R.E. 63rd Division.		Y.C.A.
189 Inf Brigade.		Y.C.A.

Confidential

Volume XVIII
Vol 16

War Diary.

31st Divisional Signal Company R.E.

June 1917.

Army Form C. 2118

WAR DIARY
or
INTELLIGENCE SUMMARY
(Erase heading not required.)

31st Div. Signal Coy R.E.

Place	Date	Hour	Summary of Events and Information	Remarks and references to Appendices
VILLERS CHATEL	1st 2nd		Normal work; cleaning, packing all wagons &c	
	3rd		Ten men sent to 13th Corps Signal School for four weeks course of training. To Whitley Brigade sub. Section.	
	4th to 10th		93rd Inf. Bde. exchange accommodation with 92nd Inf. Bde. Normal routine work; Divisional Commander inspected Company on 8th inst.	
9½ Rebreuve	11th		31st Division relieve 63rd R.N. Division in the Gavrelle Sector. D.H.Q. close at VILLERS CHATEL at 10 A.M. and open at 95 B 38 at same hour. 92nd Bde. in Reserve Area. 93rd Bde. in Right Section. 94th Bde in Left Section.	
	12th		Signal office opened at St. Catherine's for disposal of local traffic. Four wooden terminal posts erected outside signal office at D.H.Q. and cables from airlines buried into signal office.	
	13th 14th		Normal work; improvements effected in local circuits.	
	15th 18th		Laying trunk cable route in communication trenches and 9th Bde. Commenced wiring Left Sector for Offnus Wire Station.	

Army Form C. 2118

WAR DIARY
or
INTELLIGENCE SUMMARY
(Erase heading not required.)

Instructions regarding War Diaries and Intelligence Summaries are contained in F. S. Regs., Part II. and the Staff Manual respectively. Title Pages will be prepared in manuscript.

Place	Date	Hour	Summary of Events and Information	Remarks and references to Appendices
ROCLINCOURT	June 19		92nd Bde relieved 94th Bde. Batteries laying main trunks in communication trenches.	
"	20 to 26		Preparing for attack by 94 Bde on 28th.	
"	27.		94 Bde relieved 92 Bde.	
"	28.		94 Bde attacks gaining all objectives. Communication scheme Appendix 23 gives results.	App. 23. App. 24. report on Appendix 24
"	29.		Normal work.	
"	30.		ditto. Appendix 25 shows traffic diagram for June.	A/p/s 25.

M.J. MacMajor BrigR.
O.C. 31 Signal Coy R.E.

APPENDIX "C".   Page ___

SIGNAL ARRANGEMENTS.

TELEPHONE & TELEGRAPH.

(1). In addition to the normal system of lines to Battalions, a main trunk route is being constructed from S K at B 22.b.5.7 down TYNE ALLEY to a Bde. Forward Signal Station in Old German Front Line at about B 24 c.9.3. From this point lines will be laid to the various Battalion H.Q.

This main route will be maintained by two Linesmen, test points being in BAILLEUL EAST Post and junction of TYNE ALLEY AND NORTH TYNE ALLEY, in addition to S.K. and I.M.

An additional line to the central Battalions and Right Battalion will be laid down from S.K. down the railway line. Lateral lines between Battalions will also be provided. The Main Trunk Line will take precedence over all other lines as regards maintenance.

(2). BATTALION LINES.

Each Assaulting Battalion will lay two lines from its Headquarters to a point in the Front Line about the centre of its sector, whence they will be carried forward across No Man's Land by slightly different routes to the German front line. A linesman's test point for maintaining these lines will be established by each Battalion at the point where the lines enter our present Front Line.

The Right Battalion will also be in telephonic communication with THE WINDMILL.

(3). INSTRUMENTS. For telegraphic work, Fullerphones will be used. Speaking will be on D 3 telephones, and separate speaking lines will be provided.

(4). POWER BUZZERS. There will be a Power Buzzer and Amplifier at the Bde Forward Signal Station, working to the set at present at Left Battn. Hdqrs. which works to Brigade H.Q.

The Power Buzzer at THE WINDMILL will remain at its present position. The Left) Cwmtre Battalion will take over one Power Buzzer and establish it in the German front line, and work to the Amplifier at the Bde Forward Signal Station.

(5). WIRELESS. A trench wireless set will be installed at the Bde Forward Signal Station working to a similar set at Bde H.Q.

(6). VISUAL. The two Centre Battalions will take over one daylight signalling lamp, and work to the Brigade O.P. in OUSE Trench which will be in telephonic communication with Bde H.Q. B 29 b 7.9.

(7) PIGEONS. Each Battalion Headquarters will have four birds, and a reserve supply will be kept at Bde Forward Signal Station.

(8). RUNNERS. Runner relay Posts will be established at Bde Forward Signal Station and all linesmen test points,

App. "C" (cont.)

9. **CABLE DUMP.** Cable Dumps will be established at Bde Forward Signal Station, and at Brigade Headquarters.

10. Officers may use the telephone at any of the Relay Points.

    Telegrams may be sent by any Officer from any Signal Officer, but not from the Relay Points.

    Sealed packets may be handed in at any Signal Office or Relay Post.

11. From Zero hour onwards sealed packets will be sent from Bde to Battns and vice versa every hour. Battalions will collect sealed packets from Brigade Forward Signal Station hourly at half past the hour.

12. A Map showing all Telephone Stations and Relay Points is attached. *(Brigade Units only.)*

13. All Runner Posts and Relay Points will be marked with a blue and white notice board, giving the telephone call of the station.

22.6.17.

Captain,
Brigade Major,
94 Infantry Bde.

Issued to all recipients of "Instructions."

Appendix. 24

REPORT ON COMMUNICATIONS DURING OPERATIONS ON JUNE 28th 1917

All wires, telephone and telegraph, from Division to Brigades were normal and uninterrupted.
Beyond slight alterations to existing wires the only additional line arranged for was a direct telephone from General Staff Office to Brigade Major of attacking Brigade.

Arrangements at 24th Brigade.

Telephone and Telegraph.

5 pairs of wires were laid to the Brigade forward station at B 24 c 9.2 and from there were carried on to Battalion Headquarters. For purposes of maintainence etc 3 pairs were concentrated down TYNE TRENCH, the other 2 pairs being "overland" by different routes.
All wires were working correctly up till 7 p.m., having remained intact during enemy bombardment shortly after 5 p.m. At 7 p.m. all wires were cut, forward of test point at B 28 b 5.8, except the pair to the left Battalion, which went by different routes and this remained through until 10 p.m.
Communication by wire was not properly re-established to all battalions until 11 a.m. on the 29th, but telegraph was re-established to Brigade forward station at 7-30 p.m. on the 28th, though speaking to Battalions was not satisfactory, and this only for a short time.
This long delay in getting the wires through appears to have been owing, not so much to heavy barrage, but to intermittent shelling along the forward end of TYNE TRENCH where, in the first instance about 800 yards of wire was smashed to pieces, and although this portion was relaid, it was broken as the work was being done. This fact is corroborated by Lieut Guy, who reconnoitered the route after daylight.
Lieut Guy and Lieut Smith, about 11-30 p.m., personally supervised the laying of a new direct line to Centre Battalion Headquarters, but report that it was repeatedly smashed by shell fire as it was laid out, and was useless.
The R.F.A. Brigade - Battalion liaison lines were similarly cut and blown about in the same localities.

Wireless.

" CW " sets for communication between Brigade and Brigade forward station were working satisfactorily until about 6 p.m., when they were so disturbed by atmospherics caused by lightning, that they were unable to exchange signals until about 2 a.m. on the 29th.

Power Buzzers.

These were working well during the afternoon prior to the attack, but the receiving portions were damaged by lightning. The set at the Brigade forward station was in communication with the WINDMILL the whole time and got into communication with the Power Buzzer sent across to CADORNA TRENCH at 2 a.m.
The earth wires were also badly cut.

Runners.   More satisfactory.

Contact Patrol.
                    The Contact Patrol aeroplane,
in spite of very bad weather, dropped successfully
a total of four messages at both Brigade and
Divisional Headquarters at about 8.30 p.m. 10 p.m.
5 a.m. and 8.45 a.m.

Visual.
                    No messages received.   Of the
two lamps sent forward with Infantry, one is known
to have been blown up and about the other, I have
not as yet been able to ascertain what became of it.
                    Signalling lamp with left centre
liaison officer was also destroyed by shell fire.

                                [signature]

                                Major
            O.C. 51st Divl Signal Company R.E.

30.5.1917

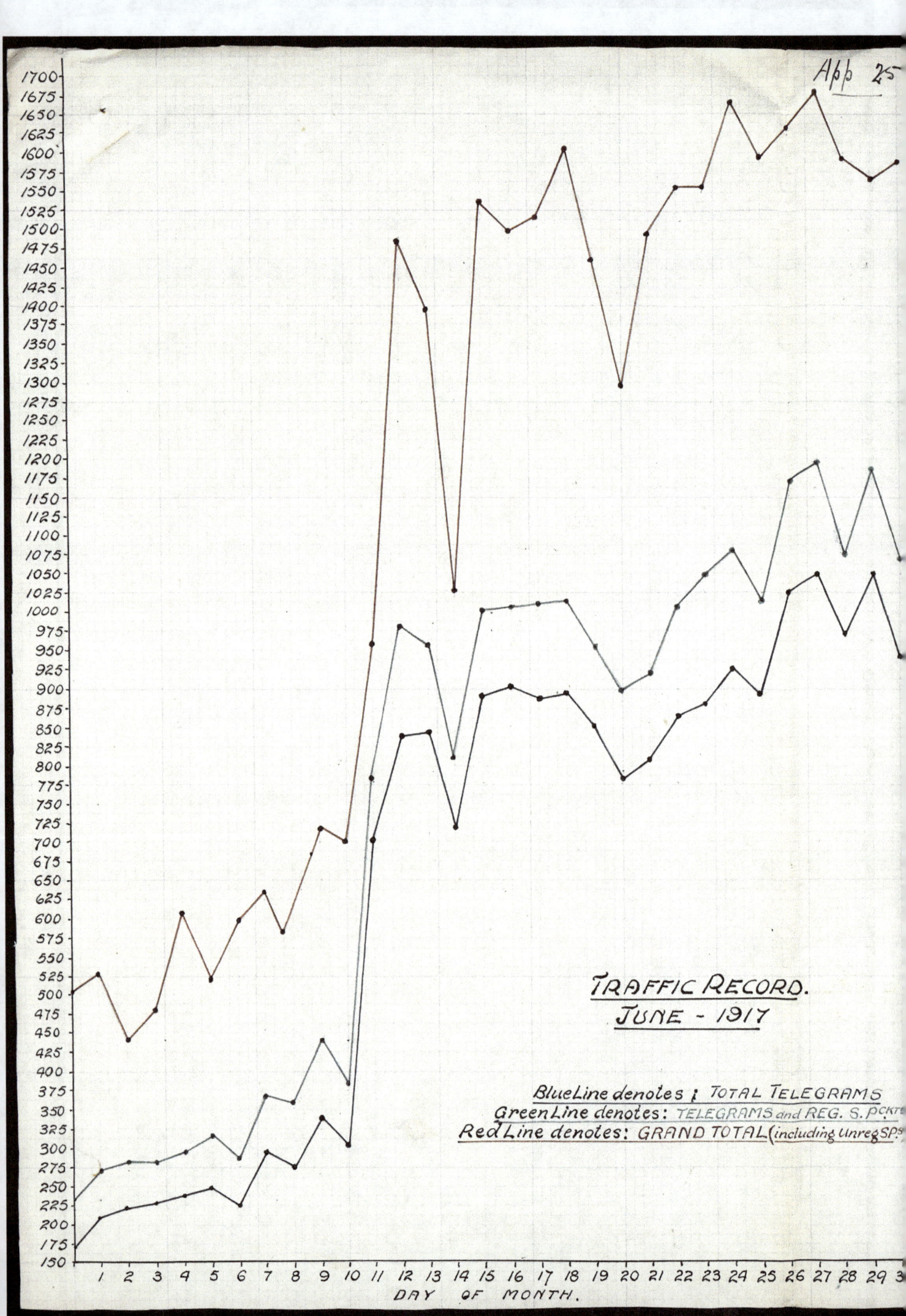

Confidential

Volume XIX
Vol 17

War Diary

31st Divisional Signal Coy. R.E.

July 1917

Army Form C. 2118.

WAR DIARY
or
INTELLIGENCE SUMMARY.

(Erase heading not required.)

31st DIV. SIGNAL COY. R.E.

Place	Date	Hour	Summary of Events and Information	Remarks and references to Appendices
ROCLINCOURT	1st		92nd Bde relieved 94th in the Line.	
"	2nd		Normal work.	
"	3rd		Night 3rd/4th 188 Bde relieved 93rd Bde – 93rd Bde being relieved by 63rd Div.	31 Dtg
"	4th		31 D.H.Q. closed ROCLINCOURT 10 a.m. & MAROEUIL 9a.m. 9th K.R.R. to MAROEUIL	31 Dtg
VILLERS CHATEL			Arrived VILLERS CHATEL 10 a.m. 9th K.R.R. moved to VILLERS CHATEL. Divn. H.Q. 31 Div moved to VILLERS. Capt. & Major. T.A.F.MAIR	
	5th		PLATTS, M.R.E. arrived to relieve Capt / Major to Latter being	
			ord. E. YORK R. in command of Signal Coy.	
			under orders to proceed to England.	
	6th		Capt. MAIR left for England leaving the Company & PLATTS	
			by Course of training to instill drill ability & etc. amongst recent reinforcements introduces Course	
	9th		3 men from each section (36 men) commenced 3 day course of training as pigeoneers at Corps. HQ.	

WAR DIARY
or
INTELLIGENCE SUMMARY

Army Form C. 2118.

Place	Date	Hour	Summary of Events and Information 31 DIV SIGNAL Coy RE	Remarks and references to Appendices
VILLERS-CHATEL	July 7th		One 2nd. Cpl. & 8 office telegraphists of the company commenced course in Rontes at XIII Corps school. Three men will form Salvage Wireless section this month.	
	11		H.M. King George visited the Div. Two lieutenants started to 6th Army Div Sig. School & others. All information re buried cables in their sectors.	
	12		The Full station and battery A.D. Station moved to FORT GEORGE (15th Hsrs. D.H.Q.) to prepare communications at 31st Div. Nights 12/13 Cpl 19 Opls commenced move H.Q 15th Yorkshire Bn. 3 men from each Brigade (3 in all) commenced 3 day course in trenching at Corps Sch. Nights 13/14 92nd & 94th Bde completed relief of 3rd Guards Bde. 31 Div HQ closed at VINERS CHATEL 10 AM and opened at FORT GEORGE 10 A.M. relieving I CAV. DIV. — Hel ARTILLERY.	
FORT GEORGE	14		F3 Bde moved to MONT ST EAOY	

Army Form C. 2118.

WAR DIARY
or
INTELLIGENCE SUMMARY.
(Erase heading not required.)

Instructions regarding War Diaries and Intelligence Summaries are contained in F. S. Regs., Part II. and the Staff Manual respectively. Title pages will be prepared in manuscript.

Place	Date	Hour	Summary of Events and Information	Remarks and references to Appendices
FM GHQ	JULY		31 DIV SIGNAL Co R.E.	
	15		WIRELESS SETS erected at Divnl HQrs and Bde HQrs for working to Corps Directing Station & also between HQrs	
	16		POWER BUZZERS issued to 93rd Bde.	
	17		CW WIRELESS sets issued at 92nd Bde ...	
	18		Routine work	
	19		— do —	
	20		— do —	
	21		94th Inf Bde relieved by 3rd Inf Bde on the night of 21/22. 94th Inf Bde to Etrehem & Grog.	
22-23			Routine work	
	24		4 Officers & 14 men of 94th Bde commenced 4 day Telephone Course at XIII Corps Signal School.	

Army Form C. 2118.

WAR DIARY
or
INTELLIGENCE SUMMARY.
(Erase heading not required.)

Instructions regarding War Diaries and Intelligence Summaries are contained in F. S. Regs., Part II. and the Staff Manual respectively. Title pages will be prepared in manuscript.

Summary of Events and Information 3rd Div. Signal Coy R.E.

Place	Date	Hour	Summary of Events and Information	Remarks and references to Appendices
Fort George			JULY.	
	25th to 28th		Routine work. Included retubing trestle on line route from W. to T. and points	
	29th		93rd Inf. Bde. relieve 92nd Inf Bde in left section. 92nd Inf. Bde. move to Château D'Acq. 94th Inf. Bde. relieve 93rd Inf. Bde in the right section.	
	30th		Routine work	
	31st		Four Officers & fourteen men from 93rd Inf Bde. commence four days course at XIII Corps Signal School. Traffic chart for month of July attached herewith.	

J. Parkinson Capt. R.E.
For O.C. 3rd Div Signal Coy.

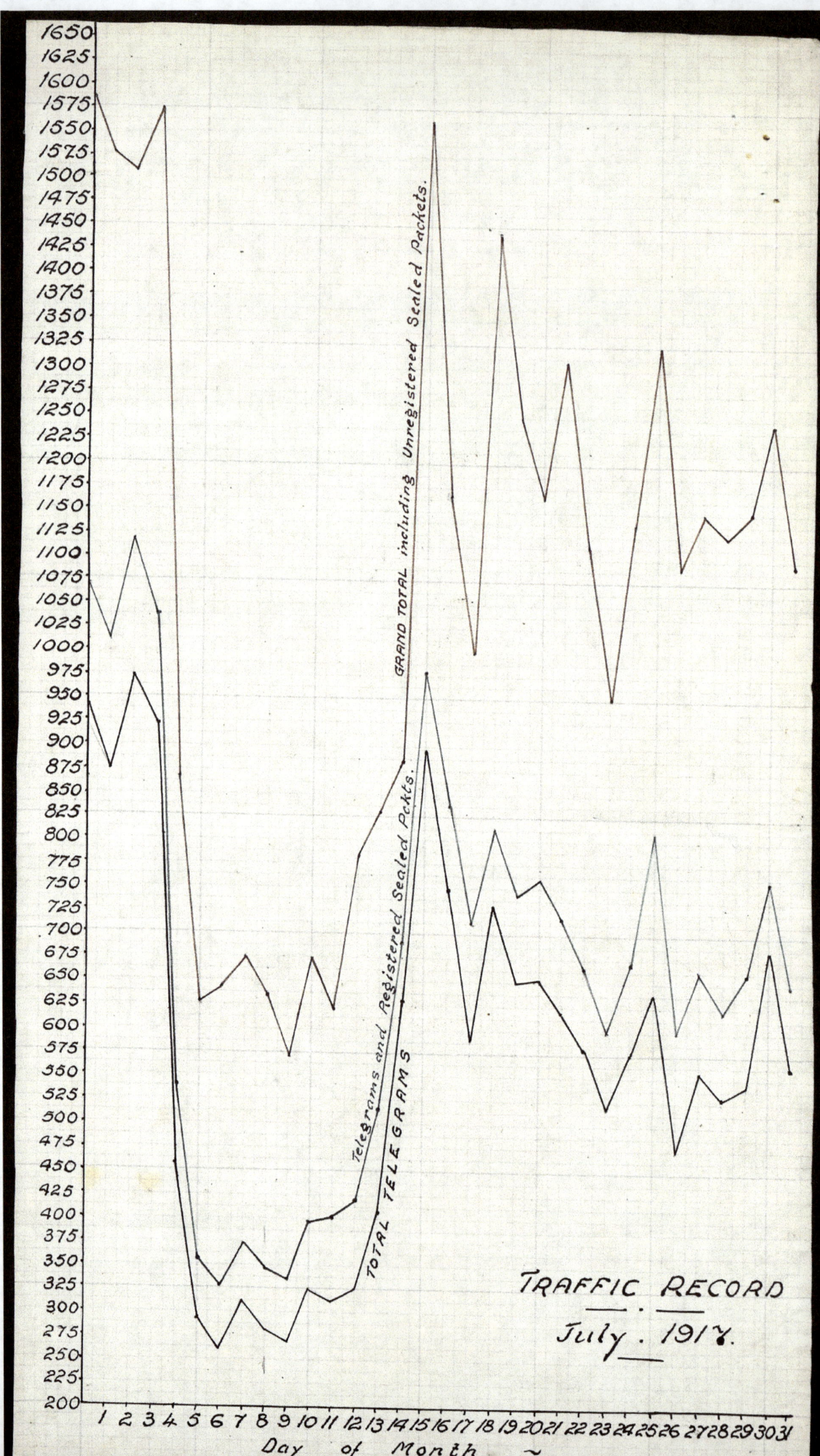

Army Form C. 2118.

Vol 18

WAR DIARY
or
INTELLIGENCE SUMMARY.
(Erase heading not required.)

31st Divisional Coy R.E.

Place	Date	Hour	Summary of Events and Information	Remarks and references to Appendices
Fort George	AUGUST.			
	1st		"Rebel all lines" notice boards fixed at following trench junctions:- T29b.15.05, T29b.8.8, T22d.9.3, T28b.4.7, T16c.89, T20a.9.9.	
	2nd		Normal routine work	
	3rd		Third site for works hors standing fixed	
	4th		New position calls received from Corps & issued by staff to come into operation at 12 noon on the 5th inst.	
	5th		Emote on Instructions regarding Communications in the Burgen gow received from Straneh & issued by us to all concerned.	
	6th		Arrangements made to commence buried cable from T.S. to Z4; digging party of 150 obtained from Brigade in reserve	
	7th		Work on works hors standing commenced.	
	8th		Digging party on above mentioned buried cable commenced work by night.	
	9th		Party from Army Wireless School return to duty on completion of course	
	10th		Normal work	
	11th		Midday post to Corps altered at their request from 12 noon to 11-30 A.M.	

Army Form C. 2118.

WAR DIARY
or
INTELLIGENCE SUMMARY.
(Erase heading not required.)

Instructions regarding War Diaries and Intelligence Summaries are contained in F. S. Regs., Part II. and the Staff Manual respectively. Title pages will be prepared in manuscript.

Place	Date	Hour	Summary of Events and Information	Remarks and references to Appendices
FORT GEORGE	AUGUST		31st Div. Signal Coy.	
	12th		Normal routine work	
	13th		2.20 p.m. 25 pain announced antis. Raid in area, turned outcome, covering party provided by 93rd Inf. Bde. team work on cable trench	
	14th to 19th		Work on new signal office at F.12.A.5.5 in preparation of following move. Work in progress daily on whole line standing. "koalas" erected for new camps. Work resumed on cable by 13th Inf. Bde.	
	20th			
	21st		D.H.Q moved from F6c (tel George) to F.12.A.5.5. at 6.30 A.M. 6 taxi for 50 men (inchansi) for 6 weeks course commences at Corps Signal School, Onville.	XIII
	22nd		Normal work	
	23rd		— do —	
	24th		On night of 24/25. 94th Bde. from Div. Reserve relieved 93rd Bde. in right sector. 93rd Bde. relieve 92nd Bde. in left sector; 92nd Bde. to Divisional reserve.	
	25th		L/Cpl. Allenby sent on Veterinary Course at Abbeville. 2/Lt. Judd & 12 L/Cpl. Boys Wormerly & 16th West Yorks sent for Course at Dunchalt Training Depot.	

Army Form C. 2118.

WAR DIARY
or
INTELLIGENCE SUMMARY.
(Erase heading not required.)

31st Div. Signal Coy.

Place	Date	Hour	Summary of Events and Information	Remarks and references to Appendices
F12A55			AUGUST.	
	26th		Normal routine work	
	27th			
	28th			
	29th		Demonstration of S.S.148 at First Army School of Signalling.	
	30th		Normal routine work.	
	31st		Traffic Record for month of August attached.	

J Parkinson Capt.
for O.C. 31st Div. Signal Coy.

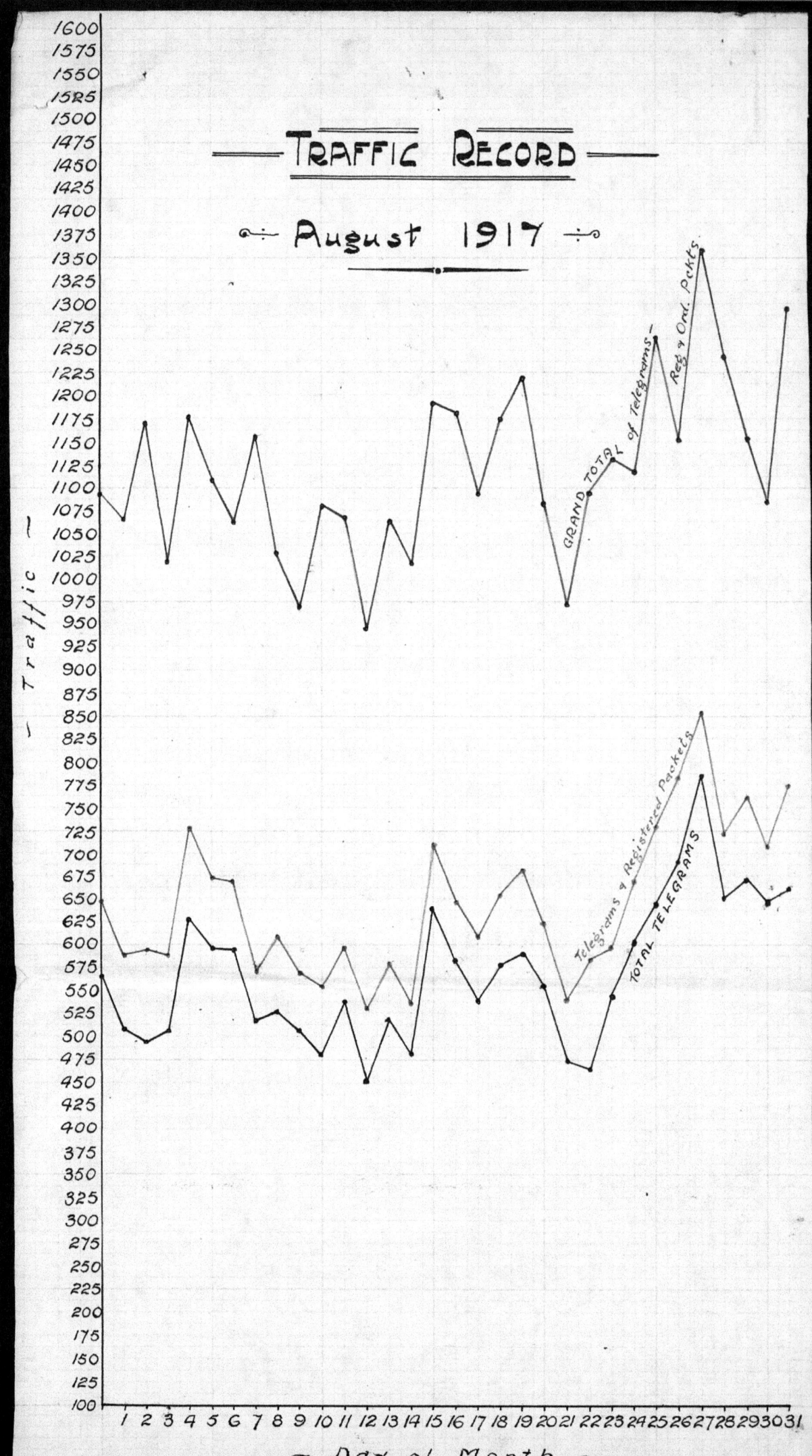

Confidential

Volume XXI
War 19

War Diary.

Headquarters 31st Divisional Signal Coy.

September 1917.

Army Form C. 2118.

WAR DIARY
or
INTELLIGENCE SUMMARY.
(Erase heading not required.)

31st B. in August - Oct.

Place	Date	Hour	Summary of Events and Information	Remarks and references to Appendices
F.12.A.5.5.	September 1st		Normal Work.	
	2nd		92nd Inf. Bde. moves from Graham O'Reg. to W.ter Stone Rgmt. & B.Bn.	
	3rd			
	4th		Preparation in connection with forthcoming move.	
	5th			
	6th			
A.29.A.34.	7th		31 Div. H.Q. moved from F.12.A.5.5. to A.29.A.34. relieving 5th Div. at 10 A.M.	
	8th		D. Signals worked Company in afternoon.	
	9th		92nd Inf. Bde. at B.20.B.14. & 94 Inf. Bde. at B.20.a.37. with 93 Inf. Bde.	
	10th		at W.ter Stone Rgt. & D.6.E. in Divisional Reserve.	
	11th			
	12th			
	13th			
	14th		Salvage parties at work in forward areas.	
	15th			

WAR DIARY
or
INTELLIGENCE SUMMARY.
(Erase heading not required.)

Army Form C. 2118.

Place	Date	Hour	Summary of Events and Information	Remarks and references to Appendices
AQA3H.			31st Divisional Coy R.E.	
	16th		September	
			20 men from this Coy Bn. sent to 13th Corps Signal school for 6 weeks course.	
	17th		2 N.C.Os from Company sent to 1st Army Signal school Rifles for Wireless Course 4 weeks.	
	18th		Normal work. Promotion of new signal Offrs talkween arouval H.Q. to permanent air lines.	
	19th		Corps Farian arrived from England to collect very fearful to having report.	
	20th		Work on Divid cable trench commenced by no Company of reserve Brigade.	
	21st		— do —	
	22nd		— do —	
	23rd		— do —	
	24th		O/ Wood attached from 18th Div'l Sig.Co. for wireless working sent to Wireless school Athieule for 6 weeks course	
	25th		Normal work.	
	26th		4. 4. O. of do. g. H.O. ferries trial tpllen in cable trench.	

Army Form C. 2118.

WAR DIARY
or
INTELLIGENCE SUMMARY.
(Erase heading not required.)

Place	Date	Hour	Summary of Events and Information	Remarks and references to Appendices
A29A3,4	September		31st Div Signal Coy B.C.	
	27th 28th		Normal work. Lieu Watts reported for duty from 2nd Div.	
	29th		Laid 220 yds. of 40 pairs in Cable trench.	
	30th		Normal work. Traffic chart for month attached.	

J. Garveison Capt.
for O.C. 31st Div. Signal Coy R.E.

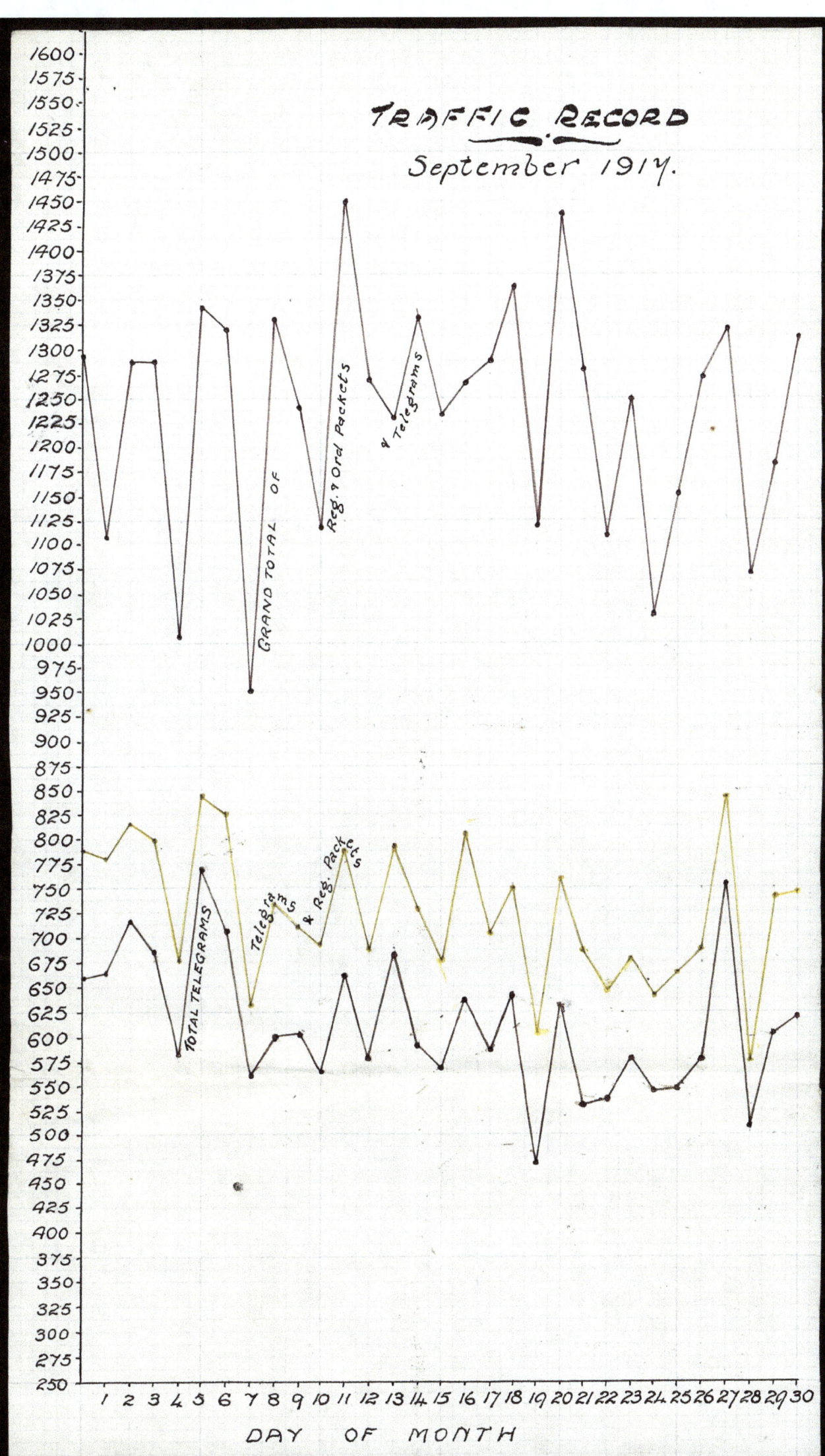

Confidential

Volume XX

Vol 20

War Diary.

31st Divisional Signal Coy R.E.

October 1917.

Army Form C. 2118.

WAR DIARY
or
INTELLIGENCE SUMMARY.

(Erase heading not required.)

31st Div Signal Coy RE

Place	Date	Hour	Summary of Events and Information	Remarks and references to Appendices
H29a 3.4	October			
	1st		Normal work. Clearing old trenches around D.H.Q.	
	2nd			
	3rd		Move completed into new dugout office	
	4th		Normal routine work	
	5th		New 3o line exchange fitted in dugout office. 57th Division (3rd Battalions) relieving 2nd Divisions	
	6th		Cable glazing arm fitted on R.T.E. route.	
	7th		New instruction issued to all concerned re Gno B.Coral messages.	
	8th			
	9th		Normal routine work. Cable construction seriously impaired interference with by severe gales & heavy rains.	
	10th			
	11th			
	12th		D.H. exchange shell struck. Personnel withdrawn from P.N. dug out. 92nd Inf. Bde. relieved by 93rd Inf Bde in right sector.	
	13th		Owing to condition of Kaves House D.R's moved in place of work operates to Bass.	

Army Form C. 2118.

WAR DIARY
or
INTELLIGENCE SUMMARY.

(Erase heading not required.)

Instructions regarding War Diaries and Intelligence Summaries are contained in F. S. Regs., Part II. and the Staff Manual respectively. Title pages will be prepared in manuscript.

Place	Date	Hour	Summary of Events and Information	Remarks and references to Appendices
A29.A.3.4.	14		[illegible handwritten entries]	
	15			
	16			
	17			
	18			
	19			
	20			
	22			
	23			

Army Form C. 2118.

WAR DIARY
or
INTELLIGENCE SUMMARY.
(Erase heading not required.)

Instructions regarding War Diaries and Intelligence Summaries are contained in F. S. Regs., Part II. and the Staff Manual respectively. Title pages will be prepared in manuscript.

Place	Date	Hour	Summary of Events and Information	Remarks and references to Appendices
Arques	24		[illegible] 31st Div Signal Coy	
	25			
	26			
	27			
	28			
	29		Lt Wood attached to company for wireless duties	
	30		On detachment of 18 cable section on training	
	31		Normal work	
			Normal routine work	

Quartermaster C/Sgt
for O.C. 31st Div Signal Coy

Confidential

Volume XXIII

No 21

War Diary.

31st Divisional Signal Coy. R.E.

November 1917.

Army Form C. 2118.

WAR DIARY
or
INTELLIGENCE SUMMARY.

(Erase heading not required.)

Instructions regarding War Diaries and Intelligence Summaries are contained in F. S. Regs., Part II. and the Staff Manual respectively. Title pages will be prepared in manuscript.

Place	Date	Hour	Summary of Events and Information	Remarks and references to Appendices
A29A.3+ ¼ Richmond	1st		31st Div Signal Coy	
	1st		Normal work.	
	2nd		Balance of Motorphones to complete establishment received from Depot.	
	3rd		One wireless detachment arrived from depot.	
	4th		Coy. with detached completed fortnights training in extra drill.	
	5th		Boys midday post sent forward and issue at 1st Regiment of B.Coys.	
	6th		Normal routine work.	
	7th		Clipping of all horses completed.	
	8th		Normal routine work	
	9th		Bu. sections transport inspected	
	10th		Normal routine work	
	11th		Common battery installed in signal office & working very successfully.	
	12th		Power buzzer personnel from Reserve Bde commence three day course at D.H.Q.	

Army Form C. 2118.

WAR DIARY
or
INTELLIGENCE SUMMARY.
(Erase heading not required.)

31st Div: Signal Coy

Place	Date	Hour	Summary of Events and Information	Remarks and references to Appendices
A29A34 N Rahincourt	13th November		2/Lieut L. Emerson joined for duty & posted to command of 93rd Bde Sig section	
	14th		Warning order received of forthcoming extension southwards of divisional front.	
			Power Buzzer course completed.	
	15th		Normal routine work	
	16th to 20th		Normal routine work; men from each section detached to attempt to be on Cable School for 10 days practical course in permanent line work	
	19th		92nd Inf Bde took over line right back front from Monchy Bala.	
	21st 22nd 23rd		Work on 92 Brigade front on improving circuits, laying on ground lines &c	
	24th to 26th		Normal routine work	

Army Form C. 2118.

WAR DIARY
or
INTELLIGENCE SUMMARY.
(Erase heading not required.)

31st Div Signal Coy

Place	Date	Hour	Summary of Events and Information	Remarks and references to Appendices
A29A34	November 29		2/Lt Emmerson to 93rd Inf Bde ordered to return til Watts on leave	
Rodricourt	30		Total ordered cable for month of November 34 miles.	

J. Emmerson Lieut
fw O.C. 31st Div Signal Coy

Confidential.

Volume XXIV

Vol 22

War Diary.

31st Divisional Signal Company. R.E.

December 1917.

Army Form C. 2118.

WAR DIARY
or
INTELLIGENCE SUMMARY.
(Erase heading not required.)

31st Div. Signal Coy

Place	Date	Hour	Summary of Events and Information	Remarks and references to Appendices
A29 A34 Rochincourt	December 1917			
	1		Normal work, additional packs for machined belts.	
	2		Warning order received of move of whole division.	
	3rd		Preparations for hand over to incoming division.	
	9th 10th		Large consignment of wireless stores received.	
	10th 11th		Divisional Area handed over to 56th Div. at 6 p.m.	
	12th		D.H.Q. Close Rochincourt at 11 A.M. reopen at Villers-Châtel same hour.	
			92nd Inf Bde. Marœuil	
			93rd —do— R.E. & Coy	
			94th —do— Trafsynkamp	
VILLERS CHÂTEL	12th		Transport section of company remain at Rochincourt.	
			Signal office removed out to Villers-Châtel.	
	10th 16		Power buzzer course for beginners held at Rochincourt.	

Army Form C. 2118.

WAR DIARY
or
INTELLIGENCE SUMMARY.
(Erase heading not required.)

Instructions regarding War Diaries and Intelligence Summaries are contained in F. S. Regs., Part II. and the Staff Manual respectively. Title pages will be prepared in manuscript.

Place	Date	Hour	Summary of Events and Information	Remarks and references to Appendices
A29 A34 Richwood	December 1917			31st Div Signal Coy
	19th		D.H.Q. went from Villers Brulin to A29 A34 refers to M.R.M.	
			94th Inf Bde over its line at Farbus Wood (H 2) + taken over Brigade pushed from 2nd Canadian Division at 6pm.	
	20		170th Bde R.F.A. alured by 251 Bde R.F.A. + took to A50 6H where they relieve the 5 Bde C.F.A at H.Pows. Communication establed with Br.D.A. exchange + sounders absent also telwell.	
	21		Repairs carried out to F.O. route damaged by enemy fire. Quiet day.	
	22		93rd Inf Bde, relieve the 167 Inf Bde H.Q. B20.6.0.4 94th do — do move H.Q. from Farbus Wood to B20.A.5.7 170th Bde R.F.A move from A6c.6.4.4 to Farbus 20 000. 165th Bde R.F.A. took right inf Bde. Communication above all establishes by phon + telegraph.	

Army Form C. 2118.

WAR DIARY
or
INTELLIGENCE SUMMARY.
(Erase heading not required.)

Instructions regarding War Diaries and Intelligence Summaries are contained in F. S. Regs., Part II. and the Staff Manual respectively. Title pages will be prepared in manuscript.

Place	Date	Hour	Summary of Events and Information	Remarks and references to Appendices
			December 1917	3rd Div. Signal Coy R.E.
A29 A34 Rosimont	23		New Code names issued for all units in the Division.	
	24		New D.R timetable brought into use & executed	
	25th		Considerable repairs required to all air line routes	
	26th		due to severe frost & snowstorms causing	
	27th		damage to same.	
	28th			
	29th		Work commenced on new buried route from Friday Hut Corn to IV	
	30		by 18th Corps Signals.	
	31st		New orders issued by G Branch relative to Gen. Attacks &c	

Jn. Dickinson Capt.
for O.C. 3rd Div. Signal Coy

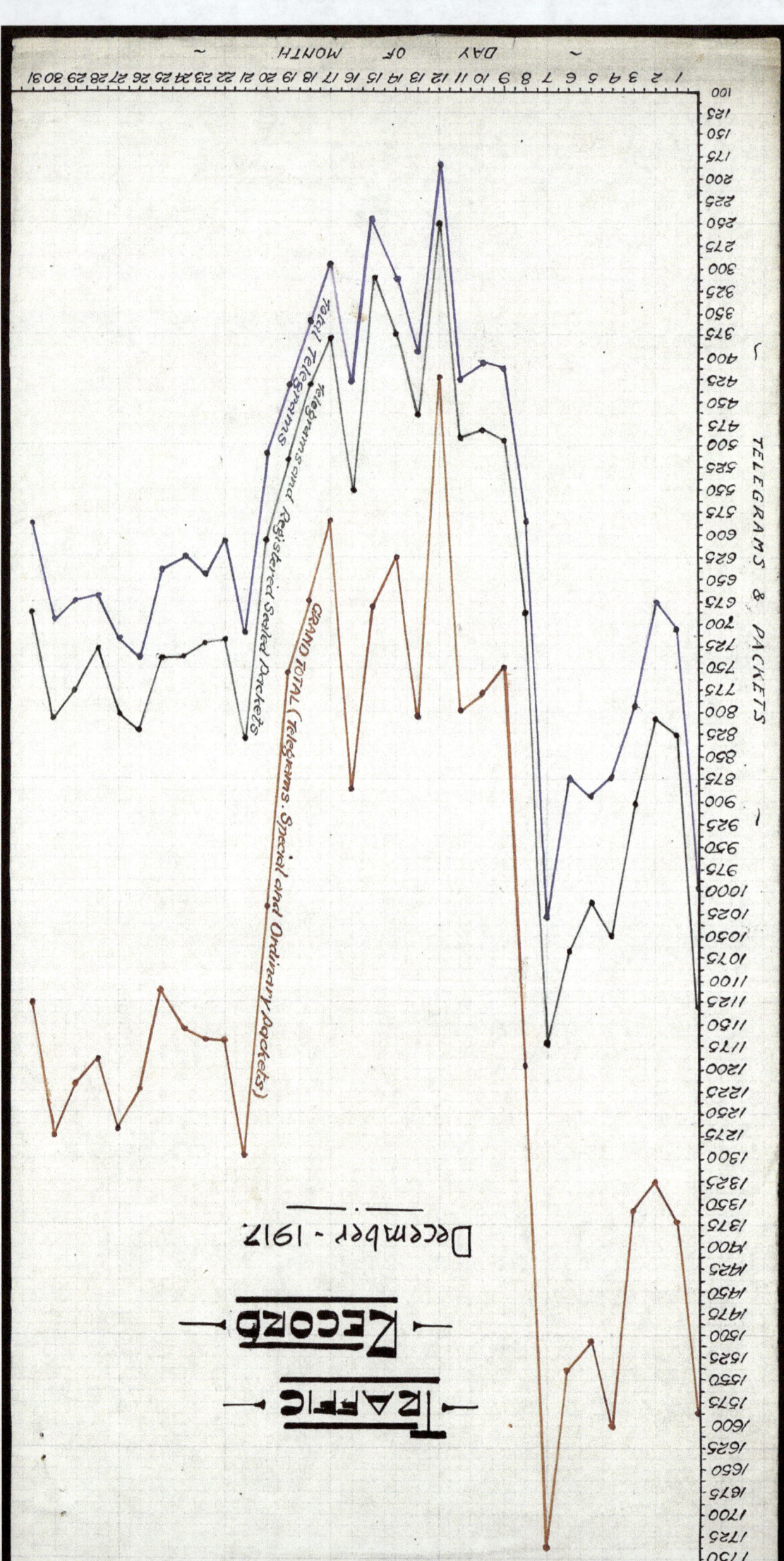

Army Form C. 2118.

WAR DIARY
or
INTELLIGENCE SUMMARY.
(Erase heading not required.)

WU 23

31st Div. Signal Coy

Place	Date	Hour	Summary of Events and Information	Remarks and references to Appendices
A29 A 3.4. Rocleincourt	January 1918			
	1		Normal work.	
	2		Lecture given to artill. Company on Trench ring telephones.	
	3		92nd Inf. Bde. relieve 93rd Inf. Bde. in Right Sector, 92nd Inf. Bde. 2 Bn. in reserve.	
	4			
	5		Normal routine work.	
	6		C/Watts to No 5 Squadron RFC for five day course in "Contact Patrol".	
	7		Lt. G.H. Neasson 1st Bn. Signal Coy returned from 1/9 Dn Australian.	
	8		Eng Snipson left unit for Cadet school England.	
			Capper Donnely left unit for Cadet School AS & 13th Bn D.gast.	
			56th Div. on our right relieved by 62nd Div.	
			Normal routine work.	
	9		Gov. Crowell to 1st Army for three weeks course in "upkeep of wireless instruments."	
	10		One reinforcement arrive from depot.	

Army Form C. 2118.

WAR DIARY
or
INTELLIGENCE SUMMARY.
(Erase heading not required.)

Place	Date	Hour	Summary of Events and Information	Remarks and references to Appendices
HqA34 Richmond	January 1916		31st Div April 1917	
	11		Sapper Duce from Wireless returned Beyond Base Cubicle returns to duty. P.E.L. set fitted with poles at Aveso.	
	12 } 13 }		Normal routine work	
	14		Sgt Pritchard reports from Signal Depot posted to 15 section	
	15		Brighter than canvas damage to French line and snow prevented works.	
	16		Maintenance taken over of PO-PZ lines, also Artillery lines.	
	17		Normal routine work	
	18		Sapper Linnman reports for duty. C/Watts to Advanced Signal Depot on Wireless Course	
	19		C. Manton attached to 93rd Inf. Bn section in absence of C. Watts on Course.	

WAR DIARY
INTELLIGENCE SUMMARY

Army Form C. 2118.

31 Divisional Coy

Place	Date	Hour	Summary of Events and Information	Remarks and references to Appendices
A29A3+ Roclincourt			January 1918	
	20		Normal routine work.	
	21		Lt. Ryanson attached to 93rd Inf Bde. section & Lt. Emerson attached to 93rd Inf Bde. section.	
	22		Sgt Brown reverts to company & 2nd Lt Quin? transferred to H.Q. from No 2 section.	
	23		Party of men under N.C.O. commenced repairs to the tel/graph from R.D. to P.Z. Burial route.	
	24		Normal routine work	
	25		Party of our signallers from teams Battalion commenced relieving ours at wood P.O.(tel/pom)	
	26		Local enemy commenced from Signal Office to Friday tel/line No. 2.B. joined 3ft. deep.	
	27		Work continued as usual	

Army Form C. 2118.

WAR DIARY
or
INTELLIGENCE SUMMARY.
(Erase heading not required.)

Instructions regarding War Diaries and Intelligence Summaries are contained in F. S. Regs., Part II. and the Staff Manual respectively. Title pages will be prepared in manuscript.

Place	Date	Hour	Summary of Events and Information	Remarks and references to Appendices
Agny & Ronville			January 1918 31st Div Sgnl Co.	
	27		92nd Inf Bde relieved 93rd Inf Bde in the RH8 sector.	
	28		Lt Emerson attached to 5th Squadron RFC for one weeks course on Contact Patrol.	
	29		2 NCO & AGNIERES for one week for Corps. Major Anstie RE Signals attached for instruction. Two OR from 93rd Bn Sec attacked to Instrument shop for instruction. Transport inspected by AA & QMG. Light Vickers guns Lewis guns up.	
	30		1 Pn Horsepower reported.	
	31		Wired new buried cable 3000 yds in length from main buried route to Right Sector Brigade Hqrs mature to Brass Armoured Dead (100 pr Copper Conduit buffers)	

J.H. Lead

Army Form C. 2118.

WAR DIARY
or
INTELLIGENCE SUMMARY.

(Erase heading not required.)

Place	Date	Hour	Summary of Events and Information	Remarks and references to Appendices
A 29 A 3 a Pulverin	31		January 1918	

List of Addressees on Div Sums:

GOC (2)
A/C Div
A/Q Div
A/G Bde (3)
Sigs Bde (4)
Reserve Bde

Heavy Battery (3)
Cdt Armrd Cars (2)
G Hqrs
GA
GA
A.D.M.S.
C.R.E.
2nd Bn Artllry
3rd Y
LLC

Div
Bde
Field
Vety
Lines Sigs Hqrs
Rec. Armd
RWF
ADMS
Attach
Transport

Arora. Wt. w11865 9/M1293. 750,000. 1/17. D. D. & L., Ltd. Forms/C2118/14.

Army Form C. 2118.

WAR DIARY
or
INTELLIGENCE SUMMARY.
(Erase heading not required.)

Instructions regarding War Diaries and Intelligence Summaries are contained in F. S. Regs., Part II. and the Staff Manual respectively. Title pages will be prepared in manuscript.

Place	Date	Hour	Summary of Events and Information	Remarks and references to Appendices
729 N 34 Redmond	31		January 1919 31st Div Signal Co	
			Weather - Power Buzzer & Amplifier working in present Area	
	2		Trench Warfare Co. (1 NCO and 6/OR) left company at Isbergues for Hun [illegible] to work at Divisional HQ of [illegible] (Geo Town)	
			" " " [illegible]	
	2		C in C's (the [illegible] the 31st Division) were read with the utmost satisfaction by [illegible]	
	3		Power Buzzer & to work at Isbergues for training for [illegible] the 13 men	
	4		Amplifier " " " " at Isbergues with A1 - ready for [illegible] use [illegible] & previous return [illegible] [illegible] returns rendered battalion	

A7093. Wt. W1289/M1292 750,000. 1/17. D. D & L., Ltd. Forms/C2118/14.

WAR DIARY or INTELLIGENCE SUMMARY

Army Form C. 2118.

31 D Septemb[er]

(Erase heading not required.)

Instructions regarding War Diaries and Intelligence Summaries are contained in F.S. Regs., Part II. and the Staff Manual respectively. Title pages will be prepared in manuscript.

Place	Date	Hour	Summary of Events and Information	Remarks and references to Appendices
H29 M34 (Bertrancourt)			[1915]	
	1		30 [?] of [illegible]	
	4		Sunday. Message from Division to Infantry Bde [?] signing up on Emphasis at Battalion HQrs. Trying to have seen [?] for Chief — believed 6 A. M. taken cable their gun to the Battalion HQrs	
	5		93rd Infy Bde relieves 92nd Bde in Right sector	
	6		D. Signals G.H.A. inspection signal office in [illegible]	
	8		880 yards of new bury in Left sector completed. This in to first half point in ENROI WOOD - 119 bare electric cable and 2 armoured trench [?] 7 ft deep to [?] front.	
	9		Communication to new Left Bde new HQrs completed	

WAR DIARY
or
INTELLIGENCE SUMMARY.

(Erase heading not required.)

Army Form C. 2118.

Place	Date	Hour	Summary of Events and Information	Remarks and references to Appendices
A29 N. 34 Robecourt	February 1918		31 Div Signal Co.	
	10		Left Inf. Bde. moved to new H.Qrs. - Right Bde. occupies the trenches.	
	11		92nd Inf Bde. reorganised & consists of 10th & 11th E. Yorks & 11th East Lancs. Relieved 94th Inf Bde. in Left sector.	
	12		2 Coy. Working Party from Depot posted to 13 subd section. 94th Bde. cease to be Bde. in Divisional reserve & the duty of being certain over by 4th Gds Bde. who takes the place of 94th Inf Bde. in the Division.	
	13		Work continued on new lines which the left sector.	
	14			
	15			
	16		being laid of 4ft deep.	
	17		4 H.Qrs Bde. relieve 3rd Bde. in line.	

Army Form C. 2118.

WAR DIARY
or
INTELLIGENCE SUMMARY.
(Erase heading not required.)

31st Div. Signal Coy.

Place	Date	Hour	Summary of Events and Information	Remarks and references to Appendices
A29 A3.4 Richmond	February 1918			
	16th		2/Cpl Mackie to Course at Cable Electric Light Overseers.	
	19th		Work still continued on new wired cable scheme.	
	20th		2/Cpl Walker arrived from N.C.O's Course at Signal Depot.	
	21st		Work still continued on new wired cable scheme.	
	22nd			
	23rd			
	24th		Spr Tyson to Wireless Course at 1st Army Signal Workshops. L/Cpl Henderson returned at XIII Corps Gas School.	
	25th		Cpl Colson to N.C.O's Course Signal Depot. Spr Reach to Richmond upon Cross Signal Depot.	
	26th		Work still continued on new wired cable system, laying of all cable completed.	
	27th			

Army Form C. 2118.

WAR DIARY
or
INTELLIGENCE SUMMARY.
(Erase heading not required.)

Instructions regarding War Diaries and Intelligence Summaries are contained in F. S. Regs., Part II. and the Staff Manual respectively. Title pages will be prepared in manuscript.

Place	Date	Hour	Summary of Events and Information	Remarks and references to Appendices
A29 A34 Robicourt	February 1918 28th		93rd Inf Bde in Division were relieved by 187 Bde. F & 2/9th 93rd Inf Bde move to Fruillien	31 FBn Duenal Company

J. Parkinson Capt
for O.C. 31 Bn Signal Coy

31st Divisional Engineers.

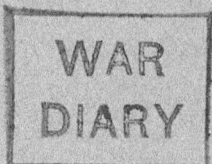

31stt. DIVISIONAL SIGNAL COMPANY

MARCH 1 9 1 8

WAR DIARY
or
INTELLIGENCE SUMMARY.
(Erase heading not required.)

Army Form C. 2118.

Place	Date	Hour	Summary of Events and Information	Remarks and references to Appendices
Beaumont	1st Feb 1918		1st Gds Bde moved [illegible] relieved [illegible] 156 & 173 Inf Bde	
August	2nd		4th Gds Bde to 1st Bde Sect	
			4th Gds Bde moved to [illegible]	
	3rd		2nd Inf Bde relieved by 156 Inf Bde in 2nd sector	
			2nd Inf Bde to 2/6	
			2nd Inf Bde moved to [illegible]	
VILLERS au FLOS	4th		2nd Inf Bde at Acqueville HQM opened at Villers au Flos [illegible] Division moved at Beaumont	
			3rd Div also at Acqueville HQ recent moved to Beaumont	
	5th		[illegible]	
	6th		Bn/Bde Coys Batn returned moved to [illegible]	
	7th		[illegible]	
	8th		[illegible]	
	9th		[illegible] Reports on [illegible] comp	

WAR DIARY
or
INTELLIGENCE SUMMARY.

Army Form C. 2118.

(Erase heading not required.)

Place	Date	Hour	Summary of Events and Information	Remarks and references to Appendices
VILLERS CHATEL	March 1916			2nd Bn Tyneside Scottish
	15th to 15th		Training in progress in platoons. Physical training maintained	
	16th		Major Ellis returned from India. Issue of clothing boots	
	17th		Box respirator drill carried out for all ranks	
	18th		Sgt Harris Coy Sergt Bruce reports from Base depot and farms Sergt Crosthe	
	19th		Farrier Sergt Crosthe to horse depot no interview	
	20th		Training programme completed.	
	21st		Warning Order to proceed to 62nd Corps Area Third Army received at 11.30 am. Orders issued for signal school to disbandoned at once.	
BASSEUX	22nd		HQ 31st Div closes at VILLERS CHATEL at 11 am, & opens at BASSEUX at 2 pm. Communication opened to 62nd Corps at Buckhamont also almost telephone. 93rd Inf Bde moved by bus to BOISLEUX AU MONT & takes over line between BOYELLES & ST LEGER.	

Army Form C. 2118.

WAR DIARY
or
INTELLIGENCE SUMMARY.
(Erase heading not required.)

31st Div. Signal Coy

Place	Date	Hour	Summary of Events and Information	Remarks and references to Appendices
BASSEUX	21st		MARCH 1918. 92nd Inf. Bde. takes up position in reserve running N along river at South End of HAMELIN COURT. 4th Gds. Bde. on Right. Below 93rd Inf. Bde. in Left Sector & 92nd Inf. Bde. in reserve holding ARMY LINE. Owing to constant move communication to Inf. Bdes. & Arty. Bdes. maintained by D.R. Wireless sets and forward communication established.	
AYETTE	23rd		31 Div H.Q. closed BASSEUX at 10 AM & opened AYETTE at 11 A.M. & opened this BOMB. COURT later. Communication to Inf. Bdes. obtained this evening. Work at once taken in hand to improve communications by laying out cable wagon and lorry routes which both well maintained & proved exceedingly useful. Frequent S.O.S. calls were passed RCD by wireless & wireless chiefly station in communication with Divy. & Bdes.	

WAR DIARY or INTELLIGENCE SUMMARY

Army Form C. 2118.

31st Div. Signal Coy R.E.

Place	Date	Hour	Summary of Events and Information	Remarks and references to Appendices
AYETTE	24		1st Sh. Bde withdrew from Hendecourt to Moyenville; communication re-established. 92nd & 93rd Inf. Bdes withdrew to Courcelles. 165 Bde. to Moyenville, 170 Bde. R.F.A. to Courcelles. D.H.Q. prepared to move to Moyenville. Visual exchange opened at 6 p.m. with three forward brigades to Ayette. D.H.Q. retired from Hendecourt to Moyenville. Poberty established at Moyenville. D.H.Q. opened at Hendecourt taking over 62nd Corps Sigs. Offus. who moved to Gro. Communication forward established with three forward brigades, to Ayette exchange where three infantry brigades & artillery brigades are now located.	
HUMBER CAMPS.	25		Forward lines to Ayette on active to Moyenville. These remain inlet to Achinsin then ground cables to Ayette.	

WAR DIARY
or
INTELLIGENCE SUMMARY.

(Erase heading not required.)

Army Form C. 2118.

Place: HUMBER BANKS

Date	Hour	Summary of Events and Information	Remarks and references to Appendices
		MARCH 1918	31st Div. August 16
26		Orders issued that no further withdrawal allowed to take place. Artillery Bdes. & Inf. Bdes. withdrew & established their Headquarters at Achiet. Communication by this forward trench still maintained.	
		D.H.Q. trying to maintain liaison outwards. Orders to evacuate Hendecourt passed to Bridge. 93rd Inf. Bde. exchange kept working at Hendecourt. All instructions sent orders were issued to return to Hendecourt when dispersed. Wire was again opened.	
27th		Arty. Bdes. & Inf. Bdes. Headquarters withdrew to Moyenneville. Forward exchange established, comms. working to Moyenly. Wireless communication failed entirely owing to Bombard. All extraction failed at Moyenly. 70 was fully forward lines.	
28th		Direct Lateral laid to Gen. Bureau. 70 Bn Regt. & Division on our right obtained Wire. Forward exchange by cable lines cut from Headcourt to this exchange.	

Army Form C. 2118.

WAR DIARY
or
INTELLIGENCE SUMMARY.
(Erase heading not required.)

Instructions regarding War Diaries and Intelligence Summaries are contained in F. S. Regs., Part II. and the Staff Manual respectively. Title pages will be prepared in manuscript.

31st Div Signal Coy

Place	Date	Hour	Summary of Events and Information	Remarks and references to Appendices
HUMBER CAMP 3.	28th		MARCH 1918	
			Owing to heavy shelling of Hannescamps & funnel communication trench being interrupted to fourteen-storey & cable was run out from VCH to Hyperly exchange & cables laid out around Hannescamps to advd posts of relief forming Bn's in village. Funnels posts station at Kurddis Hannescamps.	
			To maintenance of forward wires.	
	29th		97th Inf Bde of 32nd Div. moved into Divisional Reserve & relieved 14th HQ at Famars, communication established this forward evening.	
	30th		97th Inf Bde relieves 93rd Inf Bde in Line, 93rd Inf Bde to Fienvillers	
	31st		14th Inf Bde relieves 92nd Inf Bde.	
			96th Inf Bde resumes the Line Bde.	

J. Richardson Capt.
for O.C. 31st Div Signal Coy.

31st Divisional Engineers

31st DIVISIONAL SIGNAL COMPANY R.E.

APRIL 1918.

Army Form C. 2118.

WAR DIARY
or
INTELLIGENCE SUMMARY.
(Erase heading not required.)

Vol 26

WAR DIARY
OF

81st DIVISIONAL SIGNAL COY. R.E.

APRIL 1918

Army Form C. 2118.

WAR DIARY

INTELLIGENCE SUMMARY.

(Erase heading not required.)

Instructions regarding War Diaries and Intelligence Summaries are contained in F. S. Regs., Part II. and the Staff Manual respectively. Title pages will be prepared in manuscript.

Place	Date	Hour	Summary of Events and Information	Remarks and references to Appendices
	APRIL 1918.			
HUMBERCAMPS	1st		On completion of reliefs of Infantry Brigades, command of sector passed to G.O.C. 32nd Division. 165th Bde RFA and 170th Bde RFA remained in line under 32nd Divl Artillery. 31 Divl HQ closed at HUMBERCAMPS at 10 am and opened at LUCHEUX at noon. Communication by bell telephone established to 6th Corps and DOULLENS Exchange.	
LUCHEUX	2nd	9 am	31st DHQ closed at LUCHEUX.	
		11 am	Opened at VILLERS CHATEL under XIII Corps. Dismounted personnel of Company moved to VILLERS CHATEL by bus. 92nd Inf Bde to BAJUS; 93rd Inf Bde to FREVILLERS, 4th Guards Bde to CHELERS. Communication by sounder direct opened to 6th Corps and Inf Bdes; 92nd Inf Bde on to the 93rd Inf Bde Exchange.	
VILLERS CHATEL	3rd 4th		All Mobilisation stores overhauled and deficiencies indented for. All men's kit and equipment inspected and deficiencies issued and indented for.	
	5th 6th 7th		Class for exchange (telephone) operators started and certain linemen further trained in quick repairs of permanent routes.	
	8th		31st Divl Artillery Headquarters moved from VILLERS CHATEL to BERLES; direct telephone communication established.	
	9th		Routine work.	

Army Form C. 2118.

WAR DIARY
or
INTELLIGENCE SUMMARY.
(Erase heading not required.)

Place	Date	Hour	Summary of Events and Information	Remarks and references to Appendices
VILLERS CHATEL	Apl 10		Received orders about noon to embus, destination unknown. Dismounted personnel moved by bus, transport and lorries by road, arriving at VIEUX BERQUIN at various times between midnight and 11 am on the 11th, after a 42 miles march.	
VIEUX BERQUIN			D.H.Q. VIEUX BERQUIN, 92nd Brigade FERME LYNDE, 93rd Brigade MERRIS. The Division formed part of the XV Corps. 4th Guards Brigade moved later. 4 O.R. of 165th Bde RFA Signal Section wounded (gas.) This Bde was attached to VI Corps.	
VIEUX BERQUIN	11th	2 am	Opened Office when advance party arrived. Only communication by telephone at first consisted of one line (airline) to POO.	
		10 am	A French permanent line was repaired and put through to 92nd and 93rd Inf.Brigades, and existing airlines were connected, giving a second pair to Corps and one to 40th Division. Wireless communication was established with 92nd and 93rd Inf Bdes by 8 am.	
		11 am	The Signal Office moved to more suitable premises.	
LA MOTTE		6.30 pm	Divisional Headquarters moved to LA MOTTE. Advanced Exchange opened at farm at E 22.a.9.5. Lines in use were two permanents and one cable; YCA to YCAR. One permanent and one cable, party lines to 92nd and 93rd Inf.Bdes from YCAR; one permanent line to old 40th Divisional Exchange in VIEUX BERQUIN from YCAR, through which Exchange flank Divisions were obtained. The 93rd Brigade counter attacked successfully in the evening. Communication to Battalions was maintained throughout via Brigade Report Centre, to which the Brigade had one permanent and one cable line.	
		7 pm	4th Guards Brigade arrived at VIEUX BERQUIN. Communication established by means of one cable from Guards Brigade to YCAR and one direct to YCA. Wireless communication established from LA MOTTE to the 92nd and 93rd Inf.Bdes.	
	12th	2 pm	92nd and 93rd Inf Bdes at MERRIS. 4th Guards Brigade at LE PARADIS. Additional cable line laid from YCAR to 4th Guards Bde and on to 92nd and 93rd Inf Bdes. Wireless set at 93rd Bde moved to Guards Bde.	
		6 pm	D.H.Q. moved to LE GD HASARD. Lineman's test point (LM) established at LA MOTTE. Three permanent lines were put through from new YCA to LM.	
		7.50 pm	A cable line from BORRE, where it was considered likely YCAR would be established, was laid to YCA. It was laid round the North and West of HAZEBROUCK and a lineman's post established on it N.W. of HAZEBROUCK. Cross Roads and villages were avoided and no trouble was experienced, although the line was a long one.	

Army Form C. 2118.

WAR DIARY
or
INTELLIGENCE SUMMARY.
(Erase heading not required.)

Instructions regarding War Diaries and Intelligence Summaries are contained in F. S. Regs., Part II. and the Staff Manual respectively. Title pages will be prepared in manuscript.

Place	Date	Hour	Summary of Events and Information	Remarks and references to Appendices
	12th contd	8 pm	About 4 p.m. During the evening the 92nd and 93rd Bdes moved hurriedly to PRADELLES. YCAR was established at BORRE and 2 cables laid from PRADELLES to YCAR. 4th Guards Brigade moved to E 21 a.7-3 and took over the old YCAR at E 22 a.9.v.3 as their advanced Report Centre (ADZR). ADZ cut into two cables and the airline from LA MOTTE to old YCAR. It was found very hard to maintain these lines as they were laid along a road which was much shelled. An alternative cable line was laid from ADZR to LE PARADIS, straight across country. The communication from YCA to ADZ was maintained via this line and YCAR. Wireless through to 92nd and Guards Bdes.	
LE GD HASARD	13th	6am	La MOTTE heavily shelled. All lines in the vicinity cut and airlines down for many days. An existing cable line which had been laid by an Army Cable Section from LA MOTTE to a point a mile S.W. of MORBECQUE, was extended to YCA, giving, an alternative route. Cable line laid from YCAR to PTE SEC BOIS, to which place the 4th Guards Bde intended to move, was repaired, about midday, and extended to their present Headquarters. 4 linesmen's posts were established on this line, in order to keep it through. With the assistance of a Cable Detachment with the 34th Divisional Artillery a cable line was laid from YCA to YCAR, S.E. of HAZEBROUCK. The 92nd and 93rd Inf Bdes moved to BORRE during the afternoon. For the first time since these operations started, communication was established between the Artillery Brigades and the Infantry Brigades they were covering, though were from Brades to YCAR. The detachment with the 57th Divl Artillery laid a line from YCA to the 160th and 119th RFA Bdes and to the 64th Army F.A. Bde. The former was covering the Guards Bde. The detachment then extended this line to PTE SEC BOIS, and as the Guards Bde had by then decided not to move there, the 119th RFA Bde put this line through to YCAR. All four cable detachments and the detachments of the 57th and 34 Divl Artillery were out laying cable practically all day. Wireless was through to 92nd Bde.	
	14th	8am	92nd and 93rd Brigades relieved by the 1st Australian Division before daybreak. 4th Guards Bde moved to LE PRE a VIN, K 1 c.6-2, Sheet 36A. The cable to the old ADZ via LM was diverted to the new ADZ and extended to the 95th Inf Bde, the Brigade on the right of the Division.	

Army Form C. 2118.

WAR DIARY
or
INTELLIGENCE SUMMARY.
(Erase heading not required.)

Instructions regarding War Diaries and Intelligence Summaries are contained in F. S. Regs., Part II. and the Staff Manual respectively. Title pages will be prepared in manuscript.

Place	Date	Hour	Summary of Events and Information	Remarks and references to Appendices
LE GD HASARD	14th contd	10 pm	4th Guards Bde relieved at about 10 pm, by the 1st Australian Division. Divisional Headquarters closed at LE GD HASARD and opened at HONDEGHEM. Casualties. Killed 1 O.R. Wounded 1 O.R.	

From the 11th - 14th Sounders were used continually between Division and Brigades, as soon as the Brigade transport had arrived on the 11th. Ringing phones were used between Division and Brigades; direct when sufficient lines were available, through YCAR at other times. YCAR was not opened as a sounder office until the 92nd and 93 Bdes moved to BORRE, when operators were withdrawn from the Brigades for this purpose.
The Forward Exchange party at YCAR usually consisted of
    Lines Officer Capt G.O.Tayler M.C. G.L.
    1 B Cable Section,
    one detachment 1A Cable Section,
    a 2nd Corporal and one Office Telegraphist as Office Superintendent, and a draughtsman. The instrument repairer of 1B Section was of this party and also the operators of the Section; the latter operated the Exchange. The equipment carried in addition to the Section Mobilisation stores included:-
    1-16 line and 1-10 line Exchange
    2-4 x 3 Buzzer Units
    3 ringing telephones
    1 Sounder set
    4-12 line galvo panels.

Route diagrams were made after each change, both at YCAR and at YCA and forward to Brigades. Detachment Commanders on completing a line left route diagrams in the distant Office where the line terminated.

WAR DIARY
or
INTELLIGENCE SUMMARY.
(Erase heading not required.)

Army Form C. 2118.

Place	Date	Hour	Summary of Events and Information	Remarks and references to Appendices
			Horses and personnel were working throughout at the limit of endurance, as they had no chance of recovering from the effects of their long forced march on the first night. In nearly all the above situations the 92nd Inf Bde used a double way working Power and Amplifier set. This would not carry more than 1500 yards but was of great value. Brigades were through by telephone to their Battalions practically the whole of the time, lines laid by the Divisional Cable Section, being largely used. Hardly any visual signalling was employed. No pigeons were available. In laying cable it was found essential to avoid cross roads and villages. Light skeleton drums were found most useful for laying round these places, and the Brigades. In most cases metallic lines were laid to Battalions; single lines from Battalions forward. As a rule, each Battalion maintained a route sufficient to it's two centre Companies which were close to-gether, these lines proving of great value on more than one occasion. One Brigade Section organised it's linemen into 3 parties of 1 N.C.O. and 2 men each. This worked well, each party being always ready for laying out cable on skeleton drums. Cable lines laid straight across country gave practically no trouble, but were very difficult both to lay and to maintain if a dis occurred, owing to large ditches; the former because the line had to be pulled out; the latter because of the great difficulty experienced by linemen after dark. No time was available for reeling up lines. Practically every line laid between Division and the Brigades was taken into use for lines to Battalions when the Brigades moved back, diagrams greatly facilitating this.	

Army Form C. 2118.

WAR DIARY
or
INTELLIGENCE SUMMARY.
(Erase heading not required.)

Instructions regarding War Diaries and Intelligence Summaries are contained in F. S. Regs., Part II. and the Staff Manual respectively. Title pages will be prepared in manuscript.

Place	Date	Hour	Summary of Events and Information	Remarks and references to Appendices
HONDEGHEM	15th		92nd Brigade at V 10 c.8,8 Sheet 27. 93rd Brigade at W 13 a.5.2 Sheet 27. 4th Guards Bde at W 13 a.2.9 Superimposed Sounders to 92nd and 93rd Bdes. Permanent line extended with ½ mile of cable to 92nd Bde. Permanent line to 93rd Bde. Cable from 93rd Bde to 4th Guards Bde.	
		10.20 pm.	Cable line laid from 92nd Bde to 4th Guards Bde along cross country tracks. Permanent line superimposed sounder to BCP, 2nd Army Advanced. PCO obtained through BCP. Permanent line to HAZEBROUCK EXCHANGE (HZ.) Wireless to 92nd Bde and 4th Guards Bde. Stores overhauled and checked, and deficiencies accounted for.	
"	16th		Refitting.	
"	17th		4th Guards Bde moved to V 10 c.8,8 Sheet 27. 93rd Bde moved to HONDEGHEM. 92nd Bde composed of Composite Battalions of 92nd and 93rd Bdes. 93rd Bde composed of Headquarters only. Superimposed sounder to 92nd Bde and 4th Guards Bde. Drawing a few stores and some cable reeled up.	
"	18th		93rd Bde reformed. 8 reinforcements for Company arrived from Signal Depot. 1B Cable Section moved to AYAR as the Division had been ordered to take over from the 1st Australian Division tomorrow.	
WALLON CAPPEL.	19th		Divisional Headquarters closed at HONDEGHEM and opened at WALLON CAPPEL at noon. 92nd Bde and 4th Guards Bde relieved 2nd Australian Division Brigade in the line at 7.30 p.m. and 10 p.m. respectively, the 92nd Bde in the left sub-sector, 4th Guards Bde in the right. The 93rd Bde relieved troops in reserve at 4 p.m. with Brigade Headquarters at MORBECQUE. Signals took over at YCA and YCAR and G.O.C. assumed command of the line on completion of relief at 10 pm. Wireless communication established to 92nd Bde, 4th Guards Bde, 5th Division on right flank, 1st Australian on left flank. Visual communication established from YCA to YCAR. The existing HQ Signal Office found to be much too small and moved to a larger room. Casualties – 1 O.R. *Wounded*	
	20th		Tracing, patrolling and improving lines. Laying new cable line from YCAR to Brigades as it was found impossible to distinguish the lines in use. Visual Communication established from YCAR to 92nd Bde.	

Army Form C. 2118.

WAR DIARY
or
INTELLIGENCE SUMMARY.
(Erase heading not required.)

Instructions regarding War Diaries and Intelligence Summaries are contained in F. S. Regs., Part II. and the Staff Manual respectively. Title pages will be prepared in manuscript.

Place	Date	Hour	Summary of Events and Information	Remarks and references to Appendices
WALLON CAPPEL.	21st		Improving lines, labelling, strengthening and relaying in places. Spare lines reeled up. Capt J.Parkinson left for 13th Corps. Morning test showed all lines clear.	
	22nd		Lieut G.H.Mawson RE with 15th CCS for a few days rest. Lieut A.C.Bulmer to 92nd Bde temporarily. The Signal office again moved to a still larger room during the night 22/23rd. Casualties 1 O.R. WOUNDED	
	23rd		4th Guards Bde moved to D 17 a.5-3 Sheet 36A owing to Gas Shelling. Communication to new Headquarters established by telephone and superimposed sounder, wireless and visual. 2nd Battalion Irish Guards carried out a raid, capturing 24 prisoners. Lines from Brigade to Battalions held out well. Surplus stores left at VILLERS CHATEL collected. At one time only single cable was available so an apparatus for twisting cable was made, driven by the Lorry engine of the Electric Lighting lorry. 2 drums were attacked revolved on a spindle attached to one of the lorry wheels and the twisted cable wound on to a drum on a barrow driven from the driving shaft of the lorry.	
	24th		Improving lines and reeling up.	
	25th		Starting poling existing cable lines with hop poles collected from the BOIS de NIEPPE. Reeling up.	
	26th		Continued poling lines. Casualties 1 O.R. wounded (Gas Shell.)	
	27th		Relief by 29th Division in progress. 93rd Bde relieved and after three counter orders moved to C 11 c.5.7 Sheet 36A. Casualties. Lieut A.C.BWatts and 5 O.R. wounded (Gas Shell.)	
HONDEGHEM	28th		Morning tests during the past week have always shown all lines but one quite clear. Some trouble each day caused by traffic. The 92nd Bde and 4th Guards Bde relieved on the night of 27/28th. 92nd Bde now at V 10 a.6.0 Sheet 27. 4th Guards Bde at HONDEGHEM. D.H.Q. handed over command and opened at HONDEGHEM at 10 a.m. Telephone to all three Infantry Bdes. Superimposed sounder to 92nd and 93rd Bdes. Former line cable, latter permanent line with tee into 29th Division. Lieut G.H.Mawson returned to 92nd Bde from CCS. Lieut A.C.Bulmer proceeded for duty to 1st Army Signal School. Casualties. Nil. Lieut A.C.B.Watts to CCS.	

Army Form C. 2118.

WAR DIARY
or
INTELLIGENCE SUMMARY.

(Erase heading not required.)

Instructions regarding War Diaries and Intelligence Summaries are contained in F.S. Regs., Part II. and the Staff Manual respectively. Title pages will be prepared in manuscript.

Place	Date	Hour	Summary of Events and Information	Remarks and references to Appendices
HONDEGHEM	29th	Refitting. unobtainable.	Dumping surplus kits. Replacing cable poles with hop poles as former are O.C. visited Abbeville Signal Depot regarding N.C.O's	
	30th	Refitting.	7 reinforcements arrived, including 1 Sergeant and 1 Corporal.	

J.F. Brunwick, Capt.
for occupie 3rd Div.

Confidential

Volume XXIX

Vol 27

War Diary

31st Division Signal Coy.

From 1st to 31st May, 1918

Army Form C. 2118.

WAR DIARY
OF
INTELLIGENCE SUMMARY. 31st Divnl Signal Coy.
(Erase heading not required.)

Instructions regarding War Diaries and Intelligence
Summaries are contained in F. S. Regs., Part II,
and the Staff Manual respectively. Title pages
will be prepared in manuscript.

Place	Date	Hour	Summary of Events and Information	Remarks and references to Appendices
HONDEGHEM	1/5/18		Two direct lines put through to BCP. Line extended under orders. Only communication	
"	2/5/18		running now through BCP. Several Army lines in use as through lines. Drums. Repairing telephony.	
"	3/5/18		Repairing telephony. Rifles, etc. not on walls. List of names in Coy who can extinguish started (appendix 1). Lt J.L. Wood, 1st Yorkshire Regt. reported to Army by transit and taken on the strength from 5/1/18	A.
"	4/5/18		Collecting help from the trenches.	
"	5/5/18		Army cable buried along the telegraph route to BCP. Muddy, laborious.	
"	6/5/18		Route reconnaissance regarding running in new buried line activities communication to here, same.	
"	7/5/18 8/5/18 9/5/18		Relaying cable. Tent lashed up with a 9.2 Anna a storage to put in Column. Left the coal of Arris and front.	taking over the
		4pm 6pm	9.2 Rd. round to W.C.P. to reline & stand. Do in effect. 9.3 – Map 0	Left relay.
			Enemy Cables and ourselves had a using we called to 9.7 Rd fuse.	

A70091. Wt.W12639/M1291 750,000. 1/17. D.D & L. Ltd. Forms/C2118/11.

Army Form C. 2118.

WAR DIARY
or
INTELLIGENCE SUMMARY.
(Erase heading not required.)

Place	Date	Hour	Summary of Events and Information	Remarks and references to Appendices
Mons Bottom	13/8/18		YCAR, Enghien YCAR/YCAR. (Pacific was infiltrated through from YCA to YC2.) one from YC1 to YG2 Bde and one from YC2 Bde to YCAR. Switch line from YC1 line laid from YC1 to 2 Fanit Bn and 6.79 Bde communication laid from 6.79 Bde to 2 YC AR Cushing. This later line was run along the offside of roads where possible (it was 48 hours in so a subsequent officer survey showed many breaks Brigade Communication established from YC2 to 8th Bn HQ via YC1 & YC3. Communication from A & B Central in the memorandum. Shelter was very incomplete to one of the lines to YC4 was manufactured by Sapper and Pioneer of YC2R. Communication by buried cable established between YC3 R & 2 R of YCA 6 Central YC R & no I & I Line was mainly looked by civilian delays and improvements and offered in buried at road and gate-entries. A telephone was installed and found immediately. Shell was mainly built from retrieved village store.
Lamps likely to be stolen were removed manual. Command of estab. handed to Lft. W Diver. English completed of working and going up 2/8/18. English lines shortened between YCR to YCAR. 2/Lt. G.H. MARION RE. evacuated B.W.C.S. (sick). 2/Lt. IL was in the Rept to g 2 Rtt'x in RE in 4 M Marion.	

Appx3. Wt. W1285/9/M1291 750,000. 1/17. D. D. & L., Ltd. Forms/C2118/14.

WAR DIARY
or
INTELLIGENCE SUMMARY.
(Erase heading not required.)

Army Form C. 2118.

Place	Date	Hour	Summary of Events and Information	Remarks and references to Appendices
HONDEGHEM	11/4/18		Lc. Lund A. R.E.D. R.E. attached from Second Army Report by Lc. Lund T.B. SORROWS R.E. information officer who is not send to T_n 10.00 DMO Two lorries from 71MT YEAR hire for duties from 30 BN C/a horse 15.40 to 113 Oakes R.F.M. respectively I Railway Pumping trans Call Ri. on 31st New AUG (now Reserve During III Ord) with	
	12/4/18		20 G.S Wle Wheeler + 10 TCAR to H.Q. movements of Art. taxes no movement of difficulty expressed as with another ration supply sent of collected + sent off etc	
	13/4/18			
	14/4/18		three more to be called out	
	15/4/18		enquiry live - filling hurel + hommes with water Five lorries per day Complex received and sent to R.E. outer- (13PLV) See intelligence C	
	16/4/18		9.2 Ril relieved 9 Acs night 15/16. 9 Mech report 2 Corp arts received Kenet 9.2 See	Civ. CD TAYLOR, R.M. left
	17/4/18		Sec. UT. REED 15. Q.O.M.S. moved to WOOD (luk return Eg.)	
	20/4/18		Cir. V. Role left for Third Army - No is the small type + army mess + camp cancelled extra of service spare purchased new at 9.G Road + railway pick concealed. Two __ at Cap (or same No.)(13) Taken off to Pas Oxen in __ when in R. on Road Raits + 10 __ to 1 person to type command in by afros + outline etc.	

WAR DIARY / INTELLIGENCE SUMMARY

Army Form C. 2118.

Place	Date	Hour	Summary of Events and Information	Remarks and references to Appendices
VONDEG-M-EM	22/6/18		Lee Court L EMBRON RD commenced (with) 12/18 C.C.S.	
"	23/6/18		9.3 Bn relieved 92 Bn in front line on night of 22nd. 92 Bn to huts at W RODE MOLEN in brigade arty at square 9 Bde. Relief by 148 Bn started	
"	24/6/18		9.2 Bn moved to VIMBRES during night 23/24th. Communication with Y&R by telephone. Trench strengthening at VIMBRES by Bde in reserve from army Pioneers on 23rd.	
"	25/6/18		9.3 Bn moved to HEURHY GHEM during night 24/25th. Found rations by billet owner. Line (unbroken) manned by S.B.R. Gun stores Rn 619.	
"	26/6/18		9 am. Bn HQrs. moved to VONDEGEM & Bn relieved WARDRECQUE. 2nd Battalion in Bn in Army Reserve. Training Quietly. Generally independent training throughout area.	B
"	27th(?) 3/[?]		Training. Detail of instruction given below in appendix D attached.	

[signature]
for Lt Col
Cdg 93[?] 3rd(?)

APPENDIX A.

Subscribers 31 Div Hqrs Exchange.   2.5.18

2nd Army Advanced
15th Corps -2 lines.
Hazebrouck   223rd Field Co RE
4th Guards Bde   211th Field Co RE
92nd Bde   210th Field Co RE
93rd Bde   Staple Exchange
1st Aust Div.   1st Aust D.A.C.
29th Div.   1st Aust T.M.B.
184 Tunnelling Co RE
31st Bn.M.G.Corps.

Locals.

G.S.O. 1 Day
   do   Night   A.D.M.S.
G Branch   O.C.Signals
Q Branch   31 Div Train
G.S.O 3(night)   Signalmaster
A Mess   Message phone.
CRE
DADOS.

APPENDIX B

51ST DIVISIONAL SIGNAL COY.

COURSES

A. Cable Wagon Drill - Mounted & Dismounted.
   Hop Poling Cable.

B. Linesmen's Duties. Jointing.
   Permanent Line maintenance.

D. Instruments.

E. Wireless and Power Buzzer.

F. Visual.

G. Buzzer (for linesmen.)

H. Riding and Horse Management.

K. Exchange Operating.

J. Drill and Musketry will be carried out under Section Officers;
   Instruction of Junior N.C.O's in Communication Drill etc under C.S.M.

NOTE. Lieut Guy will supervise A. C. G. & H.
       Lieut Carnegie will supervise D & F.

Men will be tested at the end of the courses and re-rated according to their qualifications.

INSTRUCTORS

Lieut Guy. Sgt Dowie.
           Cpl MacKay.

Lieut Guy. Sgt Farrer.
           Cpl Kavanagh.

Lieut Carnegie. Sgt Read. Sgt Impet.

As arranged by Lieut Carrodus

Lieut Carnegie. Sgt Robinson.
                Cpl Page.
Lieut Guy. Cpl Torment.(Assisted
by one operator.)
C.S.M. Staff Sgt Bruce. Sgt Dowie.

Sgt Impett. L/Cpl Legg.

4. Start laying and poling of twisted D3 and single D3 cable. The cable will be laid out according to ordinary Cable Wagon Drill, poling road crossings etc, tying up on buildings. Second Detachment will follow with limbered wagon poling or tying up. On cable wagon reaching it's destination it will start back, poling and tying up until it meets rear party.

DRILL :- Spunyarn to be used in tying up on metal. All men to learn all numbers as far as possible. Nominal roll shows whether men require mainly Mounted or Dismounted training.

During morning and midday stables dismounted men will work on the wagon.

During evening stables dismounted numbers will do buzzer practice.

N.C.O's to be trained in Detachment Commanders' duties - selection of route - keep in touch with base and testing - leave diagram at linesman's posts and distant office - labelling (all lines at the same places) - test points, every 1/8th mile on poled cable, all test points at same places - map reading.

Non poling cable:- A drill to be evolved for poling two or three pairs - cable not to be strained tight - line stays on every pole to localise breaks - test points every 1/8th mile.

_____

5. Linesmen should be made to understand that their job is to keep their lines through, and to repair them in the shortest possible time when broken, and that the following notes on maintainence will help them to do this:-

Waiting linesman - equipment to be ready, cycle or horse and himself to be dressed and ready.

Location & repair of faults - Test outside office, then move quickly for ½ mile to a mile (according to nature of the line.) but a lineman should never be more than ½ hour between each tap in.

Patrolling - Improve the line every time - label.

Linesmen's reports - after patrol, stating work done and work still necessary - after repair of fault, stating position and cause.

Duties at Rest Points - Standing Orders.

Map reading.

g. (Contd.)

Jointing. - Dry insulated joint in D3 and D5 cables. Soldered insulated joint in D3 and D5 cables. Permanent line joint (iron and copper wire) - Permanent line, binding in and terminating. Buried joint in twin, quad and 7-pair. The latter in armoured, brass sheathed, lead covered, and paper core cables.

Pole Climbing.

Straining.

Location of faults on permanent line and patrolling duties similar to above.

D. Thorough understanding of the theory and working, including setting up and adjustments of the:-

        D3 Telephone
        Any type of ringing phone
        Sounder
        Transformer and Superimposing
        Test panels
        Exchanges
        Office wiring and connections

Tests of establishing complete offices with exchanges and superimposed circuits will be made during this Course.

Men will be instructed in the items laid down in the Qualification Sheet for their own trade only - e.g., Signalmen B will not be instructed in the sounder etc.

E. Erection of Stations, procedure, adjustment and operating of Trench Sets, Loop Sets, Power Buzzer and Amplifier.

Standing orders for above and general principles of wireless control.

F. Lucas Lamp (day & night) and folding shutter. This will include reading through telescope at long long ranges and under other dificult conditions such as mist, half light etc. Particular attention will be paid to station work and discipline, including transmitting stations. Divisional procedure to be used.

G. Alphabet, procedure, message form. Men must practice this in their spare time as much as possible and try to attain a speed of at least 6 words per minute.

H. Riding, grooming and feeding and horsemastership generally. Men on this course will look after their horses entirely on working and riding system, and clean their saddlery.

APPENDIX C.

MESSENGER DOGS.

Dogs were employed between Battalion and Brigade Headquarters.

Casualties were heavy. At the end of 7 days 5 dogs out of 11 had become casualties. The majority of these occurred whilst dogs were waiting at Battalion HQ.

At first the average time taken was over 40 minutes, but after six days it had been reduced to under 15 minutes.

Army Form C. 2118.

WAR DIARY
or
INTELLIGENCE SUMMARY.

51st Divisional Signal Co RE.
JUNE 1918.

(Erase heading not required.)

Instructions regarding War Diaries and Intelligence Summaries are contained in F. S. Regs., Part II. and the Staff Manual respectively. Title pages will be prepared in manuscript.

Place	Date	Hour	Summary of Events and Information	Remarks and references to Appendices
WARDRECQUES	1st		Training.	
	2nd		Training. Capt J.S.Bennett replaced Capt G.O. Tayler M.C. as Signal Officer 51st Divl Artillery.	
	3rd		Capt Tayler returned from Division to take over from Major Platts E.C.R.E.	
	4th		Training.	
	5th		O.C. (Major M.G.Platts M.C. R.E.) left for leave to England. Capt Tayler assumed command.	
	6th		Training.	
	7th		Training.	
	8th		Training.	
			G.O.C. 51st Division inspected Headquarters and No 1 Section.	
			92nd Bde moved to RACQUINGHEM area. 94th Inf Bde moved to LUMBRES area.	
	9th		Training	
	10th		Training.	
	11th		Training.	
	12th to 13th		Tests on completion of training.	
	15th	6 pm	Advanced Divisional HQ opened at EBBLINGHEM CHATEAU – U 19.c.3.7 Sheet 27.	
			92nd Inf Bde moved to area North of WALLON CAPPEL.	
			93rd " " " " South of HONDEGHEM.	
			94th " " " " South of STAPLE.	
			Communications - one line -(airline and cable) to 92nd Bde.	
			do do do 93rd Bde.	
			do do do 94th Bde. All ringing phones, superimposed Sounder. Brigades had no lines to Battalions.	
			Possible future report centres connected to YCAR by cable, one at U 17 a.2-0, the other at P 25 a.5.4. (Sheet 27.)	
EBBLINGHEM.	16th			
	17th	4 pm.	Advanced Divisional HQ closed. All lines reeled up.	
			92nd Inf Bde moved to BLAARINGHEM area, HQrs PONT ASQUIN.	
			93rd " Bde do SERCUS area, HQrs ECK HOUST CASTEEL.	
			94th " Bde do RACQUINGHE area, HQrs RACQUINGHEM.	
WARDRECQUES	18th 19th 20th		92nd Bde moved to ECCK HOUST CASTEEL.	

Army Form C. 2118.

WAR DIARY
or
INTELLIGENCE SUMMARY.
(Erase heading not required.)

Instructions regarding War Diaries and Intelligence Summaries are contained in F. S. Regs., Part II. and the Staff Manual respectively. Title pages will be prepared in manuscript.

Place	Date	Hour	Summary of Events and Information	Remarks and references to Appendices
	20/21 21st	Night	9Wrd Bde relieved Left Bde 29th Division. 94th Inf Bde moved to PONT ASQUIN. 94th Bde broken up and reformed with 24th Bn.R.W.F. 12th R.S.F. Forward Exchange 29th Division (GH) at D 7 d.8.3 taken over. (& 12th Norfolks from 74th Div.	APP. A.
	21/22 Night 22nd	10 am.	Divl Headquarters closed VANDREQUES and opened WALLON CAPPEL. G.O.C. 31st Divn took over command of Right Sector, XV Corps. Communication by Ringing phone, superimposed sounder. All lines cable, mostly D8 on the ground about 11,000 or 12,000 yards long. All lines forward through GH. There was one direct line from YCA to each Brigade in the line, and one or two spares from GH to Brigades. Lines working fairly satisfactorily, but in need of attention. GH was merely an Exchange and test point. One Cable section was kept there. Visual from GH to Left Inf Bde and to a point 1000 yards from Right Brigade. Wireless from YCA to Brigades in the line.	
	23rd			
	24th		94th Brigade relieved Reserve Brigade, 29th Division, in MORBECQUE – GD HASARD area, Brigade HQ (D 13 a.1-9. Sheet 36A.)	
	25th		94th Brigade relieved 92nd Brigade. 94th Inf Bde HQ– Le TIR ANGLAIS, D 17 a (Sheet 36A). 92nd Inf Bde to Reserve. Loop Set working from Left Bn 94th Ind Bde to 94th Ind Bde HQ. Visual (Lucas Lamp)" Right " " " " " "	
	27th 30th 22nd to 27th		92nd Inf Brigade relieved 94th Ind Bde. 94th Inf Bde HQ to D 13 a.1,9 94th Bde relieved 92nd Bde. Bde HQ to FETTLE FME D 24 a.8.2 Were spent in preparing for operations to take place on the morning of the 28th (known as (BORDERLAND) and in carrying out a preliminary operation on night 26/27th. The arrangements made and results are shown in Appendix A.	

Appendix A.

COMMUNICATIONS FOR "BORDERLAND".

DIVISIONAL.

There will be both direct telegraph and telephone circuits to the Left Brigade at GD MARQUETTE FME at E 7.b.0.0 and the Right Brigade at FETTLE FME D 24 a.7.I on existing Division and Brigade Lines.

There are also two other lines to each Brigade passing through intermediate exchanges. The Division Advanced Exchange (known as GH Exchange) is at D 7 d.6.4 and there is a small Exchange and linesman's post (known as AS Exchange) at D II d.5.7

There are direct lines from IIth Corps and 5th Division and there is also a direct line from GH Exchange to 5th Division.

Both Brigades are in wireless Communication with Division and also with each other. The right Brigade will only be able to communicate direct with the Brigade on it's right by altering it's wave length to 550 metres.

92nd BRIGADE COMMUNICATIONS.

GENERAL SYSTEM.

The general system is a main communication route from Brigade Battle Headquarters near FETTLE FARM at D 24.a.7.1 to combined Battalion Headquarters E 27 a.0.0 to Brigade Forward Station (to be established after Zero Hour during the advance) at about E 28 d.5.7. As many means as possible will be connected in this trunk i.e., Telephone, Power Buzzer and Amplifier, Runners, Pigeons and Contact Aeroplane.

LINES.

Six pairs will be laid from Brigade Battle Headquarters TO COMBINED BATN. H.QRS. (Call AB) at E 27 a.0.0. These run along four entirely separate routes, one down the LITTLE BOURRE, one down X TRACK, one through the wood SOUTH of the BOURRE and three by two different routes through SWARTENBROUCH. A permanent Exchange will be manned at AB by personnel of the Brigade Signal Section under the charge of an Officer, so that Battalions can move forward as soon as they wish to. Before Zero three pairs will be laid down entirely different routes to the SHELTERS at E 27 d.6.8, which will later be a linesman's post. A party of Signallers from the three Battalions and a Battalion Signalling Officer will be detailed to follow the last wave and extend these lines to the Brigade Forward Station(call FS) at about E 28 d.5.7 The party will establish and man this station as soon as possible. Later, when Battalion Headquarters move forward, they will be connected to this Exchange.

There is a direct line from the 95th. Brigade Advanced Headquarters (Brigade on right) at K 8 a.0.0 (Call REQD) to Brigade along the BOURRE RIVER, and the combined Battalion Headquarters at E 27 a.0.0 will have a direct line to the Brigade Forward Station of the Brigade on the Right (call BF) SLIT at K 3 d.8.9.
An existing pair through AS will be put through direct from Brigade Battle Headquarters to the 93rd Brigade on the Left.

POWER BUZZER AND AMPLIFIER.

Power Buzzers and Amplifiers will be put in at Brigade Battle Headquarters and combined Battalion Headquarters (AB) E 27 a.0.0, to work between these two stations in case the lines break down. The one at AB should also have earths out to be in communication with Advanced Brigade Headquarters on Right and also Advanced Battalion Headquarters on left at COBLEY COTTAGE, E 21 b.2.4. They should also be able to communicate with Brigade Forward Station of Brigade on Right (BF) at K 3 d.8.9.

Another Power Buzzer Amplifier will be taken forward by the Brigade Forward Station party and established at the Brigade Forward Station, E 28 d.5.7 to work back to combined Battalion Headquarters at E 27 a.0.0

If the lines are through from either FS or AB to the rear, messages brought in to either of these stations by runner will be transmitted at once by Fullerphone preferably, or DIII. If the lines are down and the message is one which can easily be put into Figure Code for use with the Popham T Panel (see SS 135 Appendix B) the Officer i/c at these offices will send it on by Power Buzzer and Amplifier in this Code, using his own discretion as to whether he sends the full message by runner in addition or not. If the Figure code is used for this purpose, map references will be sent in clear for brevity.

The attached diagram shows all the Calls in use, and Power Buzzer and Amplifier stations must be fully acquainted with these. The greatest care must be exercised not to lose the more forward of these instruments, but operators should be provided with a Mills Bomb for their destruction in case of absolute necessity.

CONTACT PATROL.

The most advanced troops will light their flares or shine their discs if there is a sun, only on the call of the 'Plane. (The call of the 'plane is a succession of A's on the Klaxon Horn, or white Very Lights.) The plane will be distinguishable by two black flappers, 12' by 18' hanging from the lower plane, and a long narrow wind vane attached to the rudder.
The Brigade Forward Station will take and put out a Battalion semi circular ground sheet with the letter W (in ground strips)

and a Popham T Panel. When Battalion Headquarters are established they will take their panel and ground sheets, and signal in the ordinary way if required, displaying their code names on the ground strips. Messages picked up by the plane from the Brigade Forward Station will be dropped at the dropping station which will be put out at Brigade Headquarters, about D 24 a.6.2, or Divisional Headquarters at U22 d.8.1

VISUAL. It will not be possible to establish Visual Communication during the Advance, but Lucas Lamps should be sent up to Companies later if they can be made use of.

PIGEONS.

24 birds will be supplied to the Brigade. These might be distributed as follows:-

6 per Battalion for distribution to Companies etc
6 for Brigade Forward Station.

The pigeons fly back to the Corps Loft at WARDRECQUES and the messages are telegraphed through the XV Corps Office at PONT ASQUIN, XV Corps and Division. Copies of these messages will be automatically sent to Division and Brigade Staffs for action if necessary as the message passes through the Signal Office.

RUNNERS.

Runner Relay Posts will be established at

the SAWMILL at E 26 b.1.9,
Combined Battn HQ at E 27 a.0.0 and at
Brigade Forward Station about E 28 d.5.7

The runner routes to Brigade Forward Station will be taped out and marked with arrows and the station itself will be marked by a notice board and a small Signalling Flag stuck in the ground. If it is necessary for the forward station to move during the operations, the tapes and arrows must be so altered as to guide runners to the new position without fail. The Officer i/c of the Brigade Forward Station and the Officer i/c at AB will be responsible for all the communications at their respective stations.

Messages from all attacking troops will be brought to the Brigade Forward Station and will be transmitted from there by the quickest means available i.e., Fullerphone, telephone, Power Buzzer Amplifier, Pigeons, Contact plane, runners, or any combination of these that the Officer i/c thinks necessary. The same applies to AB Station.

CABLE DUMP.

Eight miles of twisted D2 Cable will be dumped at the combined Battalion Headquarters (AB) E 27 d.0.0 prior to Zero, and when Battalions move forward, their Headquarters will each take two miles of this with them for laying out Company lines.

93RD BRIGADE.

The main Communication Route will be from Brigade Headquarters at GD MARQUETTE FME to Advanced Battalion HQ COBLEY COTTAGE, E 2I b.2.4 to Central Company HQ, the position of which will probably be LUG FARM, E 23 c.3.8.

This will be organised on the same lines as that of the 92nd Brigade and the same instructions apply, An Officer will be detailed to take charge of the Advanced E Station at Central Company HQ, and this station, and his duties, will correspond with those of the Brigade Forward Station of the 92nd Brigade, except that the station will be established before Zero.

LINES.

There will be three pairs by alternative routes from Brigade HQ to Advanced Battalion HQ at E 2I b.2.4 and three pairs by alternative routes from Advanced Battalion HQ to Central Company HQ. Advanced Battalion HQ will have a direct line to the combined Battalion HQ (AB) on their right at E 27 a.0.0 There is a line in existence from Post at LUG FME, E 23 c.3.8 to Company HQ at SECLIN, E 22 c.9.I This will be made use of if possible.

POWER BUZZER AND AMPLIFIER.

Will be established at Advanced Battalion HQ to work to Brigade and to another which will be established at Central Company HQ. This latter should also get into communication with the Brigade Forward Station on the Right at about E 28 d.5.7

Power Buzzer-Amplifier messages must be got through as quickly as possible so as to avoid jamming the other stations, and unnecessary calling up will not be permitted.

Separate instructions are on the attached diagram re period working if necessary.

PIGEONS.

I2 birds will be supplied to the Battalion for distribution to the Companies as required.

RUNNERS.

The main runner route will be from Central Coy HQ, LUG FME, to Advanced Battalion HQ -
(The above routes will be taped out beforehand and will be off the LA MOTTE → VIEUX BERQUIN ROAD) - thence to present Battalion HQ at E I4 d.5.3 - thence to Brigade by cycle.
Relay Posts will be established at all the above points.

CONTACT PATROL.

The instructions regarding flares are the same as for the 92nd Brigade. A Popham T Panel will be established at Central Company HQ to send messages if required. This station will be marked with a semi circular ground sheet with the letter N above it   (in ground strips.)

Messages picked up here will be dropped either at the dropping station which will be established at Brigade HQ, or Divisional Headquarters.

ARTILLERY COMMUNICATIONS.

The Artillery Communications are being issued separately. Each Brigade will have a direct liaison line to the Infantry Brigade it is covering. The 17th Brigade and the 28th A.F.A. Brigade will establish an Exchange at the combined Battalion HQ at E 27 a.0.0 and will lay lines from here to the two F.O.O's who go forward.

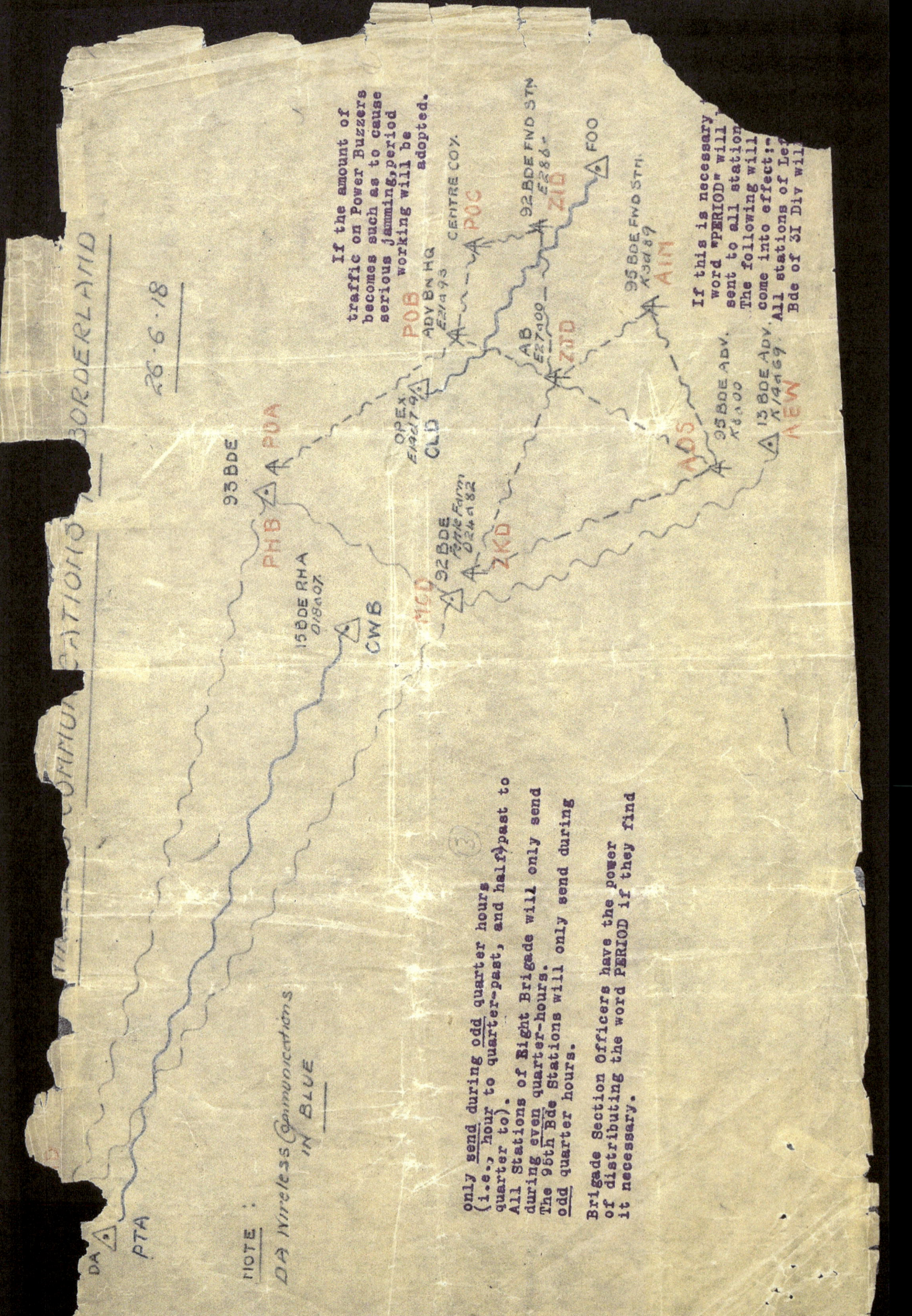

Appendix A

93RD INFANTRY BRIGADE
COMMUNICATIONS FOR THE ATTACK ON ANKLE FARM 27.6.18

The main communication route was from Bde Headquarters, Battalion Battle HQrs, Left Company HQrs, and assembly position in front line, to ANKLE FARM.

LINES. There were three pairs from Brigade to Battalion Hqrs (2000 yds), five pairs on to Battalion Battle Hqrs (1000 yds) two pairs from there via Left Company to Assembly positions (1500 yds.)

A supply of cable was dumped at assembly positions for the extension of the lines to ANKLE FARM as soon as objective had been reached.

POWER BUZZERS.

A Power Buzzer and Amplifier set was installed at Battalion Battle Hqrs to work to Brigade Hqrs (2,250 yds) and one at Left Company to work to Battalion Battle Hqrs (1,250 yds). A single Power Buzzer was sent for-ward with the assualting troops and was established in the objective (1,800 yds).

A short figure code was drawn up for use with the Power Buzzers during the operation.

RUNNERS, PIGEONS AND DOGS.

Runners, pigeons and messenger dogs were also used. Four pigeons in assault baskets, and one dog accompanied each of the two companies.

RESULTS.

Telephone communication was never entirely broken between Brigade and Battalion Battle HQ. It was found impossible to maintain cable communication forward of Battalion Battle HQ after enemy barrage started.

The objective was taken at 12.55 am. A Power Buzzer message to this effect was received at 1.8 am. One messenger dog released at 12.55 am arrived at Brigade HQ (4000 yds) at 1.51 am.

Other messages were received by Power Buzzer, Pigeons and runner during the day.

APPENDIX A

NOTES ON COMMUNICATION DURING BORDERLAND OPERATIONS.

1. **TELEPHONES.** The advanced Brigade Exchange (AB) Exchange) which was established at E 27 a.9.0 proved most useful.
   An Artillery Officer and the Machine Gun Company Commander were there with the Signal Officer who was in charge of the Exchange, and they were able to intercept and pass on to their units direct, information passing through.
   This quick method of distribution was invaluable in getting an S.O.S. through on one occasion. ~~This is the principle that has been used~~
   The Battalion Signalling Officers went forward immediately after the attack and established advanced telephones at intermediate runner relay posts about half way between the objective and Battalion HQ.

2. **CONTACT PATROL.**
   Useful messages were transmitted by means of the Popham Panel. Each took roughly half an hour between being read by the aeroplane and dropped at Divl HQ.
   It was found that the aeroplane can see the Very Lights better than the tin discs.

3. **MESSAGE DOGS.**
   Message dogs were used by the Left Brigade. Two dogs were sent forward with the assaulting troops to the objective. One of these was released at 7.17 and arrived at Brigade HQ at 7.47. This was a distance of about 5000 yards in a direct line and probably between 4 and 5 miles as the dog ran. Another dog was released at 6.40 and arrived at Brigade HQ at 8 am. Both the above dogs had to run through a very heavy barrage.
   These results show that with careful training and careful selection of the most reliable dogs valuable results may be obtained.

4. **POWER BUZZER AND AMPLIFIER.**
   These were installed in both Brigades and proved their practical value. A Power Buzzer was taken forward into the objective and a message received from there at Battalion HQrs at 6.54 am and transmitted to Brigade by 6.56 am.

5. **PIGEONS.**
   Many pigeon messages were received during the day but owing to the long distance the birds have to fly back to the loft, the information had come through by some other ~~quicker means~~ method more quickly. All birds took 40 minutes to fly and some of them as much as an hour.

APPENDIX A

NOTES ON COMMUNICATIONS OF 31 Bn Machine Gun Corps
DURING BORDERLAND OPERATIONS.

On June 27th lines were laid from Brigade Forward Exchanges to Group Commanders and thence to Batteries.

Each liaison Machine Gun Officer with the two Infantry Brigades attacking had cyclist orderlies attached to him.

Visual Communication was found impossible.

Telephonic communication was maintained on 28th between Group Commanders and their Batteries, although lines sometimes were broken. Most staions were only manned by two men.

Army Form C. 2118.

31 D Signals
Vol 29

WAR DIARY
or
INTELLIGENCE SUMMARY.
(Erase heading not required)

JULY 1918.

Place	Date	Hour	Summary of Events and Information	Remarks and references to Appendices
WALTON CAPPEL	1st		Signals Patrolling, poling and improving lines generally. Major McGill, O.C. 77th American Division attached. Preparing for move of Headquarters to hut camp a mile outside the village. 94th Inf.Brigade in Right Sub-sector - HQrs D 31 a.8.2. 93rd " " in Left Sub-sector - HQrs N 7 b.8-6 92nd Inf Bde in Reserve " HQrs D 15 a.3.9 17th Bde RFA covering Right Sub-sector, HQrs D 23 d. 7.8. 75th Bde RFA covering Left Sub-Sector D 18 a.0.7. 28th Army Brigade F.A. HQrs D 10 d.8.5. The above Artillery was under C.R.A. 29th Div Arty, HQrs WALLON CAPPEL. 29th Div Arty Sigs had a separate Exchange at WALLON CAPPEL, and a separate forward exchange in the same office as 31st Division Forward Exchange at GH. (put in for operations of 29th().) closed down. Circuit to 11th Corps (put in for operations of 29th()) closed down.	
	2nd.		31st Divl Artillery took over from 29th Divl Artillery and opened HQrs at Camp at U 23.c.8.1. 500 yards outside WALLON CAPPEL, but 31st Divl Artillery Signal Office remained in the village owing to lack of accommodation. Exchanges at GH were combined to economise personnel. All the Div.Arty Signal personnel were pooled with the rest of the Company, and the Divisional and Divisional Artillery communications controlled as one.	
	Noon 3rd.		Divl HQrs closed WALLON CAPPEL and opened U 50 c.0.7. Divl Artillery HQrs remained at U 23 c.8.1 (1000 yds away), Divl Artillery Signal Office moved to U 23 c.8.1. Divisional Signal Office established in Nissen Hut, one end of which was partitioned off to provide separate rooms for the Exchange and test room. All lines from Div.Arty were led through this office, thereby facilitating move of Divl Artillery to Div.HQrs Camp, should this be necessary during operations. Four pairs on new bury were taken into use from VCA to terminal test box near GH Exchange, this being the only buried route in the area. Lines were mainly of D5 or D8 twisted cable. They were very poorly labelled and laid unsystematically, crossing and recrossing and taking unnecessarily long routes. Nearly all the cables were on the ground and many road crossings were buried. Work was therefore immediately started to rectify this by labelling, poling and shortening lines. The lines were exceptionally long, the distance direct from Division to Brigades being 6000 to 7,500 yds. This entailed so much patrolling that it was found necessary to do away with some of the less important lines - e.g., those to Battalion Transports, all spare lines to Brigades except one to each Brigade and laterals, in order to free some men to carry on with the	

Army Form C. 2118.

WAR DIARY
or
INTELLIGENCE SUMMARY.

(Erase heading not required.)

Instructions regarding War Diaries and Intelligence Summaries are contained in F. S. Regs., Part II. and the Staff Manual respectively. Title pages will be prepared in manuscript.

Place	Date	Hour	Summary of Events and Information	Remarks and references to Appendices
			Large amount of work in the area. Four armoured twin cables, about 2000 yards long, in a ditch, were in use forward of GH. These were later extended from 2000 to 5000 yards with twin armoured cable - one pair to each infantry and Artillery Brigade in the line - about 2000 yards in ditches and 2000 yards in a canal. The joints - every 1 mile - were tied on to stakes to form test points. These cables did not prove very satisfactory, especially the old original length, which developed bad intermittent earths. Therefore, later, the cables in ditches were pulled out of the bottom of the ditch and fastened with stakes to the bank nearest the enemy, and some lengths were replaced with D5 twisted cable. Brigade and Battalion lines were mostly of light cable. In view of the length of these lines - distance Brigade to Battalion was about 2000 yds, Battalion to Company about 2000 yds - direct and the effect bad weather would probably have on them, orders were issued to replace all light cable with D8 or D5 Twisted Cable. This could only be carried out slowly owing to shortage of cable.	
	4th		Lieut J.I. Wood M.C., West Yorks Regt to COS, Sick. Lieut B.S.Tion R.E. to 92nd Bde Signal Sect.	
	4th and following days		Work indicated above continued.	
	Night 4/5th		92nd Brigade relieved 93rd Bde in Left Sub-Sector and opened HQrs at D 17 d.5.7., retaining old Brigade HQrs (93rd) as a Forward Exchange. 93rd Inf Bde to Reserve.	
	5th.		Major MacGill left - 5 Officers and 3 O.R's (Signals) also from 74th American Divn arrived for instruction. Those from Wireless Coy remained at Divl HQrs. Those from Lines Company went to Forward Exchange. Those from Outpost Coy to Brigades in line.	
	10/11th Night		93rd Bde relieved 94th Inf Bde in Right Sub-Sector; 94th Inf Bde to Reserve.	
	11th		American personnel left. Same number arrived. Distributed as on 5th.	
	14th and following days.		Preparing for move of Forward Exchange, 2000 yards further forward, to D 15 p.8.C. (new call PC). This move reduces length of lines in use by about 15 miles. It was necessary to do this to reduce patrolling so as to free men for other work, or d to simplify the system, shorten lines and clear the area of as much cable as possible.	

Army Form C. 2118.

WAR DIARY
or
INTELLIGENCE SUMMARY.
(Erase heading not required.)

Instructions regarding War Diaries and Intelligence Summaries are contained in F.S. Regs., Part II. and the Staff Manual respectively. Title pages will be prepared in manuscript.

Place	Date	Hour	Summary of Events and Information	Remarks and references to Appendices
	18th		XV Corps Cyclist Battalion (less 1 Coy) placed under orders of G.O.C. 31st Division - HQrs at D.S.d.1.3. connected to Forward Exchange.	
	Night 18/19		94th Inf Bde relieved 92nd Inf Bde in Left Sub Sector. 92nd Inf Bde to Reserve.	
	19th		Forward Exchange moved to D.U.5.b.9.-6 (Call RC). Wires and test room established in English Shelter. Two companies Cyclist Battalion placed under left Inf Bde in line. They were short of Signallers and had no instruments. The latter had to be lent to them.	re.
	20th		Further improvement of the system of lines started. It was decided to retain only three main routes from YCA to RC, these to be as direct as possible and of poled cable - except existing 2000 yards of ditched armoured cable (4 pairs.) The erection of a four pair poled cable route laterally across these three routes was started to form a grid system, and a lineman's post established at one end of the lateral route. One lineman's test point of three men, forward of RC became unnecessary owing to the shortened distance between RC and Brigades, and it was withdrawn. The diverting of forward lines to avoid above test point and other weak places, and to shorten them was begun. Reeling up lines thrown spare was started. Personnel at RC to carry out above work was organised in parties of three, each under a N.C.O. All lines to Brigades passed through RC except one line to Right Group.	
	21st and flg days.		Above work continued.	
	Night 22/23rd		92nd Inf Bde relieved 93rd Inf Bde in Right Sub Sector. 93rd Brigade to Reserve.	
	25th		Lieut B.S. Lion RE to CCS sick. 2/Lieut A. Reid RE to 92nd Inf Bde Section.	
	Night 28/29th.		93rd Inf Bde relieved 94th Inf Bde in Left Sub-Sector. 94th Inf Bde to Reserve.	
	29th		Loop sets installed at Left Group C.P. and Left Group HQrs, manned by personnel drawn from Infantry Brigade Wireless Pool, as no gunners had yet been trained.	
	31st		Right Brigade established a Forward Exchange (AB) at I.27.c.4. to economise lines and reduce maintainence.	

Army Form C. 2118.

WAR DIARY
or
INTELLIGENCE SUMMARY.
(Erase heading not required.)

Place	Date	Hour	Summary of Events and Information	Remarks and references to Appendices
			During this month it was found impossible to obtain all the stores required. Demands for cables were reduced to about a third, and only 1/3 to 2/3 of the cells, tape, labels etc indented for were supplied. Instruments - Fullerphones etc - were still short. Two Visual Buzzer Exchanges were received and issued to Brigades. They proved much quicker to operate than a 4 X B buzzer unit, but needed very careful adjustment and do not stand transport. Visual Signalling was established to all Brigades from GH, distances varied from 3000 to 4,5000 yds. Communication from GH to Divisional Signal Office was by phone direct, or by visual to AB (about half way between YCA and GH) and thence by phone. 12 men were attached from Battalions to provide visual communication to Brigades. Two of these live at GH, the remainder are under training at Divl Hqrs. Left Infantry Brigade and Left Artillery Group had communication by visual to their Battalions and Batteries, but this was impossible in the case of the Right Inf Bde and Right Artillery Group, both of which were separated from their Battalions and Batteries by a wood. Two Trench Sets were used, one at each Brigade in line, working to Wilson set at Divl Hqrs. 2 Loop sets, 2 combined Power Buzzer - Amplifier sets and 7 Power Buzzers were in use between Companies, Battalions and Brigades.	

Army Form C. 2118.

WAR DIARY
or
INTELLIGENCE SUMMARY.   51st Divisional Signal Co. RE.
August 1918

(Erase heading not required.)

Instructions regarding War Diaries and Intelligence Summaries are contained in F.S. Regs., Part II. and the Staff Manual respectively. Title pages will be prepared in manuscript.

Vol 30

Place	Date	Hour	Summary of Events and Information	Remarks and references to Appendices
Wallon Cappel	August 1st		Course lasting 10 days for 10 Divisional Artillery Signallers, in working of Loop sets started at Div. H.Q. Div. Visual party of 13 men drawn from Battalions also under training. These men were intended to provide visual communication between Division and Brigades or other Units during Mobile warfare when telephone lines could not be advantageously laid.	
	1st and following days.		Improvements of lines continued -	
	Night 4-5th		121st Inf. Bde. of 40th Div. attached for training and took over Right sub-sector of left Bde. Visual communication established to 121st H.Q., also Wireless (the Brigade brought trench sets with them) Telephonic communication established, one line direct from Bde. through R.C. Test Point to Div., from from Brigade to R.C. Exchange,-,. XV Corps Cyclist Battn Withdrawn,	
	5th		Extension of bury up to report centre and Brigades started under Corps supervision.	
	8th		Lieut H. Guy left to report at S.S.T.G. England, for tour of duty at home. Lieut D.L.Carnegie took over charge of R.C. Forward Exchange.	
	Night 9-10th		92nd Inf Bde relieved 93rd Bde. 93rd Bde to reserve.	
	9th		Discontinued replacing light cable with heavy on account of shortage of cable-.	
	11th		Cable detachment attached from 30th Div Arty. to assist in clearing the area of cable. Lieut E.J.New joined the Company. 2/Lieut W.A.Jones R.E. to R.C.Forward Exchange.	
	Night 13-14th		120th Inf Bde relieved 92nd Bde in Right Sector. 92nd Bde relieved 121st Bde in Centre Sector 94th Bde made a local attack on a one Battalion front.	
	19th		Enemy withdrawing opposite the front - battalions moving forward.	
	20th		119 Inf Bde of 40th Division moved up in support.	
	Night 21-22		G.O.C. 40th Div. assumed Command of the Sector. 51st Divisional H.Q. opened at Renescure 119th Inf Bde relieving 94th Inf Bde. Latter to Hazebrouck area in reserve, 93rd Bde relieving South African Inf Bde in 9th Div area in support. 92nd Bde remains in forward area in reserve	
	22nd 5pm		51st Div Arty. remains under 40th Div. Communication to Brigades via Division in line.	
	23rd		93rd Bde relieved 26th Inf Bde in Left Sub-sector. 92nd Bde to support.	
	25th 10am		G.O.C. 51st Div. assumed command of Left sector, H.Q. B.36.c.2.6. 9th Division to Training area office established in Nissen Hut. Wireless through to Brigades in line, Flanks and Corps. Range to Brigades - 7,000 ▼ 5,000 yards. Visual communication established through one transmitting station to all Infantry and Artillery Brigades. Lines to Brigades all ran on Bury to Annie Exchange - 4,000 yards, thence to right Brigade by overlandncable, and to Left Brigades on Bury for another 1,200 yards and then overland cable. 9th Div Arty. Office was combined with 51st Div office, the Artillery lines coming on to a 10 line, the others on to a 30 line Exchange, there was a direct line to each Infantry Bde and four trunks to Annie Exchange, (Contd)	

Army Form C. 2118.

WAR DIARY
or
INTELLIGENCE SUMMARY.

31st Divisional Signal Co. RE.
AUGUST 1918

(Erase heading not required.)

Instructions regarding War Diaries and Intelligence Summaries are contained in F. S. Regs., Part II. and the Staff Manual respectively. Title pages will be prepared in manuscript.

Place	Date	Hour	Summary of Events and Information	Remarks and references to Appendices
	25th	(Contd)	through which Exchange Div Arty got the Artillery Bdes. One line to Annie was superimposed sounder. Telegrams for Artillery Brigades were sent on sounder to "Annie" and thence by telephone. Superimposed sounder was working to both Inf Bdes in the line. Work was immediately started to improve existing lines by putting in better cable, labelling and poling (where advisable) and by altering and improving the routes of some lines. It was considered inadvisable to rely entirely on the bury - which later developed bad earth faults - so three pairs of D.8 Cable were laid to Annie Ex. and two from there forward to Left Infantry and Artillery Brigades, and the poling of these lines was started. New D.R.L.S. Time Table to Brigades, Corps, Flank Divisions and Heavy Artillery published as normal. List of Subscribers on Exchanges attached (see Appendix A)	
Following Days, Night	26th and 27-28th		Above work continued.	
	29th		The Division moved left, taking over 107 Inf Bde front of 36th Division. Brigade H.Q,rs did not move but a considerable alteration in Brigade communications was necessary. Fires observed as far back as ARMENTIERES. Enemy believed to be retiring.	
	30th		Enemy retired during night beyond BAILLEUL (a distance of 4,000 yards) 7 - pair Armoured Cable laid down from FLETRE to METEREN. Two detachments sent forward to old 93rd Brigade H.Q. 93rd Bde moved Headquarters to METEREN at 4.0pm. Div H.Q. moved at 6.0pm to old 93rd Bde H.Q. between Caestre and Fletre, and 9th Div Arty H.Q. to farm within 280 yards 45,000 yards further forward) 94th Bde withdrawn to support when BAILLEUL taken.	
	31st		Advance continued. 92nd Bde moved up to near 94th Bde. 93rd Bde moved to South edge of BAILLEUL followed by detachment laying line of D.8 Twisted Cable. Test point and Forward Exchange established on this line just West of BAILLEUL. Direct lines laid to all Brigades. 29th Div. taking over from 31st Div. - 87th Inf Bde relieving 93rd Bde. Latter withdrawing to support round BAILLEUL. Brigade H.Q. moving back to old Brigade forward Exchange between METEREN and FLETRE. Advanced Exchange and Cable detachment also moving back to Div. H.Q.	

Appendix A

SUBSCRIBERS ON TELEPHONE EXCHANGES IN 31ST DIVISIONAL AREA.

31st Divl Exchange.

G Branch	12th K.O.Y.L.I.
Q Branch	210th Field Coy.
G.O.C.	31st Divl Advanced Exchange.
G.S.O. I	XV Corps.
C.R.E.	9th Divl Artillery.
A.D.M.S.	51st Bde RFA.
A.P.M.	9th D.A.C.
31 Divl Train	2nd Army Advanced.
D.A.D.O.S.	29th Division.
92 Inf Bde	36th Division.
93 Inf Bde.	Hazebrouck.
94 (Yeo)Inf Bde.	Signal Master.
O.C. Signals.	

31st Divl Advanced Exchange.

Advanced Dressing Station	51st Bde RFA.
R.E. Dump.	9th D.T.M.O.
31st Division HQ	94th Inf Bde.
221 R.G.A.	119th Bde RFA.
9th Divl Artillery.	31 Bn M.G.Corps.
93rd Inf Bde.	
36th Division	50th Bde RFA.

93rd Brigade Exchange. (Right Bde)

31st Division	Staff Captain.
G.O.C. 93rd Bde.	31 Divl Advanced Exchange.
Brigade Major.	223rd Field Coy RE.
Signal Officer.	50th Bde RFA.
Right Bde (Flank Division.)	

94th (Yeo) Inf Bde Exchange. (Lt Bde.)

31st Division.	211th Field Co R.E.
G.O.C. Left Bde.	107th Inf Bde.
Brigade Major.	51st Bde RFA.
Brigade Details.	119th Bde A.F.A.
Signal Officer.	31 Divl Advanced Exchange.

9th Divl Artillery Exchange.

29th Divl Artillery.	Staff Captain.
31st Division.	R.A. Moss.
C.R.A. 9th Divn.	Counter Batteries.
Brigade Major.	31 Divl Advanced Exchange.

92 Bde Exchange (Reserve Bde)

Bde Maj
Staff Capt.
E.O.
Sig Off.
92 Bde Transport Off
94
31st Divn.

WAR DIARY
INTELLIGENCE SUMMARY

31 D. Sig Coy
September 1918

Place	Date	Hour	Summary of Events and Information	Remarks and references to Appendices
	1st		Division and 9th Bde Line completing Mov Stores, Salvage Cable. Brecs overhead Cables to Brigades. Gve trip PRUDE HOUSE W.5.C.39. Lines to Flank Divs. Rear units checkean on Line.	
	2nd		Brigade orders to move to an area S.of BAILLEUL. YCAN pars (cables, bins. maraguers) ran. ground to battin' eins. Amoured Cable with D. & knocke. Order cancelled later. YCAN party packer and spare office kit may towed to METEREN and BAILLEUL	
	3rd		16 &17 Bde RTS dismiss the Divisional meeting to an area near FLETRE. Gve Army Cable scheme given to Company. 31 Division park on regend fronts. scale of 29 Div — 92 Bde relieving 87 Bde (29) Div Sigs moved. YCAN rode to S.27.d.9.3 — 2000 yds S.E. of BAILLEUL. Divis'l Cable gave communication to Flanks. 10 & 92 Bdes to CRECHE on AVENUE	
	4th		supervisors carried overhead Cable Brigades to communication Cable from the precedins army to Bridges of lines to two outposts	
			Bt Supple moved to area S.of BAILLEUL and established the Gd LUNATIC ASYLUM. Communication by Cable forward. No advanced office opened at GOUGH HOUSE had improved. No advance of our line day the advance.	
	5th	5.30. to 10.5	2000yds further East — 31 Bde Army HQ's are in the Divisn'. G.O.C 31 Div'n Gen'l L Bramd and CRE an advd Stg — G.O.C end renainen of Divn Hrs remained	

WAR DIARY
or
INTELLIGENCE SUMMARY.

(Erase heading not required.)

Army Form C. 2118.

Place	Date	Hour	Summary of Events and Information	Remarks and references to Appendices
Camp	5th		PN DE HSE 12000 Yds near Superieure Number as YCA to each Infantry Bn. C.R.E. Check officer and Corps 9th Infantry Reliance 8th & 9th Infantry Left & 2/5 Sun front 93 I.B. moved to occupy 9th Infantry area again 16th & 17th I.B.s R.T.A. Ways with arrears to occupy front the under 31 I.B. 92, 93 and 94 Inf Bdes 16.5/17.0, 18/17 Bde 17.0A 119 Arm Bde 17.0A – 92, 93 – 9th Army pioneers and new lines taken over by Brigades. Enemy shelling from Y.015 to Bgade here over and heavy at Y.CA Wiped the line to Brigade here are 31 I.B. It taken over much of Indungun cable (some of the formers to laying and funders are to be Invaluable. There were a short of line to all Brigade Exempt 15 and 17 Bde 18 I.B.	
	6th	6 P.m	4.O.C 31 Divt took over command of left sub section	
	6th		Improving line. Railing 118 thousand cable 16.5 Bde 17.0 Split sub-school road 118 Pt and 6 P.R. through Leo phelong	
	7th		Nord Commanders arranged 92 and 94 Infte are changing Places (H.C) and N. EUV E G LISE have taken over Especially P.C.Os mainly due to refugees coming	
	8th		the manhands on road from Dounker	
	9th		119 I.T.A Bde withdrawn from Seaward 17th Bde 17.0 also took over S.H.P	
	9th		Poling and improving line. many Imends on former cable due to both futures any both movements	
	10th		31.9th withdrawn Y 31 Trench & mud Silence	
	11th			

WAR DIARY or INTELLIGENCE SUMMARY

Army Form C. 2118.

Place	Date	Hour	Summary of Events and Information	Remarks and references to Appendices
	12th		330 Bde RFA handed over No. 31 Div Phone Commns through 170 Bde RFA Exchange. COs opened in BAILLEUL to order such men there	
	Night 12/13	9 am	Guns No Clock at GOUGH HOUSE and others at NEW Mr. PRUDE HSE near CHESTIRE. One cable section moved to PRUDE HSE. 93 Bde Inft relieved 92 Bde Inft and opened Hd at GOUGH HSE. 15th Bde RHA + 170 Bde RFA unchanged from prev. day	
	13th		Remainder of No 10 No 1 Sections Nos 1 detachments and Guns Arty of another moved to PRUDE HOUSE 93 Bde Infte relieved 94 Bde Infte	
	Night 13/14			
	14th	Noon	Guns artillery moved to PRUDE HSE. Wgn to Y Stat MONE handed new commander of the company to Mr J'R Nairn. MONE and left of VIII Corps commencement (Give 3 mn of Guns faults and cables) Mm Y CO to PRUDE HSE (Y Cm.) Formerly (exchange is 93 Inf to office.) Sounded Y CA to 93 Inf te. Wires moved from TRENCHER by sounds to 94 Inf te and 165 + 170 Bde RFA. Another cable at the moment sound to Y CAn two wires now Major from Y CAn to Y CAn BAILLEUL EXCHANGE friendly by Army.	
	16th		Doing case and improving lines round Y CAn	
	17th		Started laying 2 pairs of Cable from Y Co to Y CAn passing of our lines installed	

WAR DIARY or INTELLIGENCE SUMMARY

Army Form C. 2118.

(Erase heading not required.)

Place	Date	Hour	Summary of Events and Information	Remarks and references to Appendices
	18th		15 WEL Zapps captured SAYER FARM. Communications and parties (signal/sappers) good during operations.	
	19th		9th Infantry relieves 93 Infantry in line	
	HQ		POPERINGHE	
	MOAS			
	19-20		Medium T.M. Batteries, 14" Bde R.H.A. reg't the Divn.	
	20th		Wiring up new Sig.ne offices in relieved CHESTRE forward to mont of Dvs HQ	
	21st		Conveying fire from 1.C.A. to YCAR from Divn Signal to 4 Inf.Bde Offices - Subordain - Field Artillery Brigades Infs to de. H.A.Bde - R.T.O. relays officers.	
	22nd		Carperson moving for new Offices	
	23rd 2.30pm		Divn HQ moved to CAMP CHESTRE Divn actively relieves PRUDE H'SE	
	24th 10AM		Div Cav Sqn moved to her CAMPON CHESTRE 92 mm hy Bde relieved 94 Bde, 94 Bde to MONDEGHEM	
	25&26th		Work on line continues	
	27		Majority of Sqns by moved to YCAR 93 Infantry moved to BAILLEUL	
			92 Infantry moved to 72.4 & 2.9 (near COURTE PREVE FARMES) Communication by new (?) Cable party laying during morning.	
	6pm			

WAR DIARY
or
INTELLIGENCE SUMMARY.
(Erase heading not required.)

Army Form C. 2118.

Place	Date	Hour	Summary of Events and Information	Remarks and references to Appendices
	28	5.30 a.m	Troops formed prior to attack. Attack preceded adv. B.Hqs. (ylam) 14TCRA opened Gough HSE and Brown HSE over wan office at both advanced Report Centre (see PRO.) Wire and Visual station opened at T.14.D.3.1. W/T through to Central Wilson topo adv. Train and EE message (auto exchange) 92,93 Infanteen teleg nos. Hqs. at EE message to transmit to a spare Wilson set. All forward wires had by cable to Brigades if necessary. 93rd Inf (500 yd) Rearle EE and Lury set now found by cable to Hd. 93rd Inf/Bde moved to T.26.a.2.9. 94 " " " " " Baileeur and later to T.26.A.2.9. Germans commenced great putting of smoke and wind clouds. Bursa gunning much trouble owing to their great severity. Flooding of these troops etc.	
	Night 28/29		93 Inf Bde advancing through 92 Inf/bde. 94 Inf/bde preceeding. Wire and cable difficulties with 93 Inf/bde commenced when 93 Inf/Bde fallen were 9am owing to teleppo wires delaying cable wagon	
	29	9am	93 Inf/Bde U10.c.2.a. 94 Inf/Bde U.14.A.1.5. B/Ck on telephone communication with JCA Wireless Sig ordered up forward owing to traffic width. New Visual Station Established on HILL 63. alls. Dr. Rear Post. Generally more Cyclists could reach all Hqs. somehow walking action connecting Hill 60 ft to	
		11.30a.m	93 Infantry adv. advancing but not extending far beyond previous Hqrs. No orders	

WAR DIARY
or
INTELLIGENCE SUMMARY.

Army Form C. 2118.

Place	Date	Hour	Summary of Events and Information	Remarks and references to Appendices
	29th Oct 1914	7pm	Corps advch HQ is returned to BLARINGHEM. Division has now returned to CAESTRE leaving 1 Bgde at Gough Hse (G.H.) 93 Inf Bde forward the line taken 2000 yds E of MESSINES and view reported by Brigade to be —	
	30th		Rear Office pulled over from Corps 160th Bde 1770 moved to T12A5.1. Orders not received to cross Bridge owing to bad state or Inshment not yet known. Tonight much have experiences a cold winter weather from map.	
	30/31	Night	94 Inf. Bde moved to BAILLEUL. Old HQ broughtup more. Bde now holding myn from 93 Inf Bde leftrear.	

J. Duncan 31/10/14

J Hanu? N.S.
C.M.G Staff 31st Divn

WAR DIARY
INTELLIGENCE SUMMARY.
(Erase heading not required.)

31 Div Signal October 1918. Army Form C.2118.

WW 32

Place	Date	Hour	Summary of Events and Information	Remarks and references to Appendices
	1st	6 am	330 Bde RFA. ceased to be under CRA 31st Div.	
	4/5th	night	93 Inf Bde took over whole Divisional front, 92 Inf Bde moved to Support. Owing to length of communication, Brigades were not always possible from Divl H.Qrs at CAESTRE to Brigades in the line.	
	6/7th	night	94 Inf Bde relieved the 93rd Inf Bde, 93 Bde to Support. 92 Inf Bde to Divisional Reserve.	
	12/13th	night	92 Inf Bde relieved 94 Inf Bde, 94 Bde moved to Divisional Reserve. During the above period recovering overland cables was considerably impeded - shortened, poled etc - and the buried lines in part put into better order and preparation made for a further advance.	
	15th	9.30 am	Advanced Divl H.Qrs opened at HYDE PARK CORNER near the Inf Bde in the line. Enemy withdrawal probable.	
	16th		92 Inf Bde advancing, Brigade HQrs moved to West bank of the LYS, and later further East to near QUESNOY	
	17th		92 Bde still advancing, 93 Inf Bde moved forward E of the LYS, to near QUESNOY. 94 Inf Bde moved to and W of the LYS. Communication by wire, with leading Brigade, failed for three hours owing to supply of cable being held up by traffic block at the bridge over the LYS. During this time Visual and Wireless were both used successfully. 170 and 64 Bdes RFA moved across the LYS. Communication to them was through the Inf Bde with which	

Army Form C. 2118.

WAR DIARY
or
INTELLIGENCE SUMMARY.
(Erase heading not required.)

Instructions regarding War Diaries and Intelligence Summaries are contained in F. S. Regs., Part II. and the Staff Manual respectively. Title pages will be prepared in manuscript.

Place	Date	Hour	Summary of Events and Information	Remarks and references to Appendices
	17th Cont.		they were working. The OC Signals of Infantry and Artillery Brigade worked together; the former manning a control office, the latter seeing to the laying of lines. Usually 1 line was run forward to a combined Brigade Advanced Exchange and Battalion etc. connected to this. Similarly one line (twisted D cable) was laid by cable detachment from Division to Div Adv. Exchange which was kept near to the forward Brigade. The Bde were connected to this exchange and all lines superimposed. Sounders This worked well except that it was found impossible to maintain an adequate supply of twisted cable although fibre transport was worked to its limit. It was impossible to use the lorry as no lorry bridges were available.	
	18th		165 Bde RFA moved to CAESTRE to CAPPELLEM — communication through Corps. 92 Inf Bde advancing beyond TOURCOING. Speech with leading Brigade becoming impossible but telegraphic communication maintained — intermittently owing to moves. 93 Bde to TOURCOING. 94 Bde to QUESNOY and	
	19th Noon		Div HQrs moved to CROIX BLANCHE. Line & visual communication through to Brigades, also visual to leading Brigade through two transmitting stations. Communication to 15th Corps was direct or line to 94 Inf Bde when part to PCO was vindod and connected through a transformer to the Div-Bde line. DC Sounder was worked to PCO, telegram for 94 Bde having	

WAR DIARY or INTELLIGENCE SUMMARY

Army Form C. 2118.

Place	Date	Hour	Summary of Events and Information	Remarks and references to Appendices
	19th (cont.)		to be gotten. These have held until Corps Commander Report Centre was opened later. 92 Inf. Bde. (H.Qrs. NATTRELOS) advanced and slightly and landed over their front to the 14th Division. 93 Bde relieved the 40th Division, south of 92 Bde, and advanced their line east of ROUBAIX. Communication maintained by through the town. Great difficulty experienced at first by DRs in finding Brigade H.Qrs.	
	20th		94 Inf Bde moved to LANNOY. 93 Inf Bde reached the line of the ESCAUT. H.Qrs at NECHIN. Communication to Brigades by cable, wireless, and visual and motor cyclist.	
	21st	10am	Div. H.Qrs moved to LANNOY. Following week - improving cable lines, and riding up in area just passed. Clearing up fighting	
	25th		move to relieve 29th + 9th Divisions in 2nd Corps area. 31 Div 2 being relieved by 40 Division. Communication to Brigades by DR until connected to 29th or 9th Div. took longer on arrival.	
	26/27 (night)		92 Inf Bde relieved two Brigades of the 9th Division in the line. H.Qrs VICHTE.	
	27th	10am	31 Div H.Qrs moved to N. edge of COURTRAI looking over from 27 Div 31 Div artillery H.Qrs opened at STACEGHEM, relieving 29 D.A. 165 RFA Bde and medium TM Batteries now only one of the Division	
		noon	31 Div took over command of old 9th Div front. 94 Inf Bde	

WAR DIARY
or
INTELLIGENCE SUMMARY.
(Erase heading not required.)

Army Form C. 2118.

Place	Date	Hour	Summary of Events and Information	Remarks and references to Appendices
	27th (Cont:)		Arrived at DEERLYCK (in Support). Div Advanced Exchange established at DEERLYCK Chateau and two lines laid from Division to this. Lines handed from there forward (9th Bde to Brigades). Wires erected here to transmit to Brigades.	
	28th.	10am	93rd Inf Bde to STAGEGHEM area in Reserve. 31 Div Artillery took over Artillery Command of the front from 9th Div Arty. 28 Bde RFA under CRA 31st Div. Difficulty experienced in establishing normal communication to Brig Bdes owing to mist. This was however successfully accomplished during a clearer interval. Long range Lucas lamps found most useful and worked well for 6000 yards during daylight.	
	29/30th (night)		94 Bde relieved 92 Bde in the line. Later to support. Preparing for another advance.	
	30th		Advanced Exchange moved to VICHTE Chateau. Much difficulty experienced in maintaining communication here owing to shelling.	
	31st	5.25 AM	Advanced Div HQrs for G Branch and Div Artillery opened at VICHTE Chateau, also 92 & 91 Bde HQrs. Attack by 94 Bde started. 94 Bde HQ moved forward during the night and further during the day. When later, move took place, a second Div Advanced Exchange was opened at the HQrs 94 Bde left.	

Army Form C. 2118.

WAR DIARY
or
INTELLIGENCE SUMMARY.

(Erase heading not required.)

Instructions regarding War Diaries and Intelligence Summaries are contained in F.S. Regs., Part II. and the Staff Manual respectively. Title pages will be prepared in manuscript.

Place	Date	Hour	Summary of Events and Information	Remarks and references to Appendices
	31st (Cont)		Communication by cable established from Hr(RC Exchange) to 94 Inf Bde, 28, 50, 165 & 170 Arty Bdes and two lines taken over from Year (VICHTE) to RC. Great difficulty experienced with traffic when one of these lines was down. Wireless & Visual from VICHTE forward were of considerable assistance. Much trouble experienced on lines from VICHTE to rear HQrs, believed to be due to enemy agents, the wires being mainly down over, in several cases in one dug only. Vandl from VICHTE to Rear Offices, also of considerable use on account of this. Dropping Station at Div Advanced & used frequently at one period of the attack. 50 Bde RFA withdrawn from the Division.	

J.H. Burnie Hawk

For Jn a n Cody, that Signal Co.

WAR DIARY
or
INTELLIGENCE SUMMARY.

Army Form C. 2118.

Stafford C.C. Nov 1918   No. 33

Place	Date	Hour	Summary of Events and Information	Remarks and references to Appendices
COURTRAI	1		Div. HQrs at COURTRAI and Billets Bn at VERTE MOULIN	
	2		Bn march from hospital Coiffé relieved Bn under canvas	
	3	1130	Infantry & Artillery Bde. near G.KERICH	
	4		A.G. Hd. Moved COURTRAH support HCD Zoom A.S.	
	5		B.A.C.	
	6	94 a.c.	[illegible] what only [illegible]	
			Arty. Brig. Bde. Artillery reli[illegible]	
			Coy. 61st Batty/HER Arty HOORNE 32nd Bde & [illegible] at Bas	
	7	1700	M.G.B. no HOORNE Ch G Coy & R Bn 1500	
			Ran Thu third of SHELDAHEM	
	8	1500	Div. HQrs closed RENOO & opened at SNELLEGHEM also Co.	
			of Brigades in NEATHOUT BOSCH	
	9		Adv. by French troops in RUDDE	
	10	n.m.	Div. HQrs closed SNELLEGHEM and R.U.VERTE	
			[illegible]	
			Rem. Div. HQ. [illegible]	
			Le [illegible] at [illegible] RAMX	

WAR DIARY
INTELLIGENCE SUMMARY

Army Form C. 2118.

31st Div H.Q. Cy
Nov 1918 Part II

Place	Date	Hour	Summary of Events and Information	Remarks and references to Appendices
RONEN RENAIX	11	10.30	Officer i/c H.Q. closed at RONEN this a.m. & March of Coy from RENAIX to QUATRE VENTS. Armistice signed. Whole Coy mans moved to Brigade artillery in readiness at 11.00. Rode to Bruges (via 35 Div) any by Coy Comdr & 4 Subalterns as per GMO returning.	
	12		Photos being up.	
	13		My. Ramsay returned from Brig. Warren of command.	
			Visit from 2 men back of COURTRAI staying at RUYEN SNEISSEN	
	14		Ditto	
COURTRAI	15	11.00	Bde H.Q. about WARENAIX trekked to POTTELBERG, COURTRAI at 1100hrs.	
	16		Clearing of communications	
	17		Ditto	
	23		Company traced Relative claims from meeting amongst K.O.Y.L.I.	
	24		H.Q. Coy supplied to the BLANDECQUES to stay 3 nights amp-lin. BOUSBECQUE, BAILLEUL, CASSEL	
ST OMER	25	08.00	Arrived St. Omer in 3hrs. Nights halt at BLANDECQUES at Chateau Roy	
	26		H.Q. arriving Chateau	
	27		Party on leave to England	
	30		Details sent to England, where remainder of Coy is stationed	

WAR DIARY. 31st Div Sig. Coy.

Dec. 1918.

PLACE	DATE	HOUR	SUMMARY OF EVENTS AND INFORMATION.	REMARKS.
BLENDECQUES	1	-	Div HQ at Blendecques. 92 Bde at Blendecques, 94 Bde at Tatinghem. Div Arty at Wizernes. 93 Bde at Wizernes. 31 M.G.C. at Lumbres. Other Units in St. Omer. Communication with St. Omer Units via 92 Bde. All communication arranged over open wire routes with O.C. Signals, St Omer. Company busy cleaning harness and wagons, and overhauling equipment generally.	
"	2	-	Education classes started, and carried on successfully throughout the month. Canteen and Recreation Room opened. Outdoor recreation also taken up with enthusiasm. Association football matches arranged with other units in the Div.	
"	17th	-	94 Bde moved to LUMBRES. Communication arranged at foot via LUMBRES exchange, but later a direct line was arranged to 94 Bde Exchange, and telephones were	

WAR DIARY

31st Div. Sig. Coy.
Decr 1918. Sheet 2.

PLACE.	DATE	HOUR	SUMMARY OF EVENTS AND INFORMATION	REMARKS
	17th Wed.	—	obtained via 94 Rly, instead of via LUMBRES.	
BLENDECQUES.	18th	2 p.m.	The G.O.C. inspected the Company, and presented medal ribbons to those who had won awards.	
"	21st	—	Education classes suspended; to be re-continued Jan 2nd.	

[signature]
Capt. R.E.
M.O.C. 31st Div. Sig. Coy. R.E.

Army Form C. 2118.

WAR DIARY
or
INTELLIGENCE SUMMARY.
(Erase heading not required.)

Place	Date	Hour	Summary of Events and Information	Remarks and references to Appendices
Aundergem	4th	—	Education Classes re-commenced. Attendance good	
	6th		9th. The moved to 5th Army Staging Camp Anderlecht, communication being established with 19th Corps.	
	11th		Owing to demobilisation of two instructors on this date, all Educational classes (except French and Shorthand) came to an abrupt termination, no more instructors being available.
The results of the inspection by the Committee for Quarter ending Dec 1918, showed that the Coy still retained its previous good record for efficiency in transport, again leading the list on its premier place since the inauguration of this competition.
During the month two parties, each consisting of 12 men in charge of an officer were sent to Brussels for the purpose of taking cake. A large amount of cable in good condition was recovered, dumps being formed on	

www.ingramcontent.com/pod-product-compliance
Lightning Source LLC
Chambersburg PA
CBHW08085123O426
43662CB00013B/2072